WRITING SKILLS CURRICULUM LI

JACK UMSTATTER

Illustrations by Maureen Umstatter

THE CENTER FOR APPLIED
RESEARCH IN EDUCATION
West Nyack, New York 10994

Library of Congress Cataloging-in-Publication Data

Umstatter, Jack.
Writing skills curriculum library / Umstatter, Jack.
p. cm.
Contents: Unit 1. Ready-to-use word activities
ISBN 0-87628-482-9
1. English language—Composition and exercises—Study and teaching (Secondary)—United States. 2 Education, Secondary—Activity programs—United States. I. Title.
LB1631.U49 1999
808'.042'0712—dc21 99-21556
CIP



*Printed in the United States of America*

10 9 8 7 6 5 4 3 2 1

ISBN 0-87628-482-9



**The Center for Applied Research in Education**
West Nyack, NY 10994

**http://www.phdirect.com**

# DEDICATED

To my wife, Chris, for your many years of love and support.
Your words have always meant so much. Thanks for everything.

# ACKNOWLEDGMENTS

Thanks to my wife, Chris, for her many hours of dedicated work in this subject and to my daughter, Maureen, for her artistic creativity.

Thanks again to Connie Kallback and Win Huppuch for their support and encouragement with this series.

Appreciation and thanks to Diane Turso for her meticulous development and copyediting and to Mariann Hutlak, production editor, for her tireless attention to this project.

A special thanks to my students, past and present, who inspire these ideas and activities.

Thanks to Terry from WISCO COMPUTING of Wisconsin Rapids, Wisconsin for his programs.

Definitions for certain words are taken from *Webster's New World Dictionary, Third College Edition* (New York: Simon & Schuster, Inc., 1988).

# ABOUT THE AUTHOR

Jack Umstatter has taught English on both the junior high and senior high school levels since 1972, and education and literature at Dowling College (Oakdale, New York) for the past nine years. He currently teaches English in the Cold Spring Harbor School District in New York.

Mr. Umstatter graduated from Manhattan College with a B.A. in English and completed his M.A. in English at S.U.N.Y.—Stony Brook. He earned his Educational Administration degree at Long Island University.

Mr. Umstatter has been selected Teacher of the Year several times and was elected to *Who's Who Among America's Teachers*. Most recently, he appeared in *Contemporary Authors*. Mr. Umstatter has taught all levels of secondary English classes including the Honors and Advanced Placement classes. As coach of the high school's Academic team, the Brainstormers, he led the team in capturing the Long Island and New York State championships when competing in the American Scholastic Competition Network National Tournament of Champions in Lake Forest, Illinois.

Mr. Umstatter's other publications include *Hooked On Literature!* (1994), *201 Ready-to-Use Word Games for the English Classroom* (1994), *Brain Games!* (1996), and *Hooked on English!* (1997), all published by The Center for Applied Research in Education.

# ABOUT THE WRITING SKILLS CURRICULUM LIBRARY

According to William Faulkner, a writer needs three things—experience, observation, and imagination. As teachers, we know that our students certainly have these essentials. Adolescents love to express themselves in different ways. Writing is undoubtedly one of these modes of expression. We stand before potential novelists, poets, playwrights, columnists, essayists, and satirists (no comment!). How to tap these possibilities is our task.

The six-unit *Writing Skills Curriculum Library* was created to help your students learn the elements of effective writing and enjoy the experience at the same time. This series of progressive, reproducible activities will instruct your students in the various elements of the writing process as it fosters an appreciation for the writing craft. These stimulating and creative activities also serve as skill-reinforcement tools. Additionally, since the lesson preparation has already been done, you will be able to concentrate on guiding your students instead of having to create, develop, and sequence writing exercises.

- Unit 1, *Ready-to-Use Word Activities*, concentrates on the importance of word selection and exactness in the writing process. William Somerset Maugham said, "Words have weight, sound and appearance; it is only by considering these that you can write a sentence that is good to look at and good to listen to." Activities featuring connotations, denotations, prefixes, roots, suffixes, synonyms, antonyms, and expressions will assist your students in becoming more conscientious and selective "verbivores," as Richard Lederer would call them. Diction, syntax, and specificity are also emphasized here.

- The renowned essayist, philosopher and poet, Ralph Waldo Emerson, commented on the necessity of writing effective sentences. He said, "For a few golden sentences we will turn over and actually read a volume of four or five hundred pages." Knowing the essentials of the cogent sentence is the focus of the Unit 2, *Ready-to-Use Sentence Activities*. Here a thorough examination of subjects, predicates, complements, types of sentences, phrases, clauses, punctuation, capitalization, and agreement situations can be found. Problems including faulty subordination, wordiness, split infinitives, dangling modifiers, faulty transition, and ambiguity are also addressed within these activities.

- "Every man speaks and writes with the intent to be understood." Samuel Johnson obviously recognized the essence of an effective paragraph. Unit 3, *Ready-to-Use Paragraph Writing Activities*, leads the students through the steps of writing clear, convincing paragraphs. Starting with brainstorming techniques, these activities also emphasize the importance of selecting an appropriate paragraph form, organizing the paragraph, introducing the paragraph, utilizing relevant supporting ideas, and concluding the paragraph. Details on writing various types of paragraphs—description, exemplification, process, cause and effect, comparison–contrast, analogy, persuasion, and definition—are included.

- "General and abstract ideas are the source of the greatest errors of mankind." Jean-Jacques Rousseau's words befit Unit 4, *Ready-to-Use Prewriting & Organization Activities*, for here the emphasis is on gathering and using information intelligently. Activities include sources of information, categorization, topics and sub-topics, summaries, outlines, details, thesis statements, term paper ideas, and formats.

- "Most people won't realize that writing is a craft." Katherine Anne Porter's words could be the fifth unit's title. Unit 5, *Ready-to-Use Revision & Proofreading Activities*, guides the students through the problem areas of writing. Troublesome areas such as verb tense, words often confused, superfluity, double negatives, and clarity issues are presented in interesting and innovative ways. Students will become better proofreaders as they learn to utilize the same methods used by professional writers.

- "Our appreciation of fine writing will always be in proportion to its real difficulty and its apparent ease." Charles Caleb Colton must have been listening in as Unit 6, *Ready-to-Use Portfolio Development Activities*, was developed. Students are exposed to many different types of practical writings including literary analyses, original stories and sketches, narratives, reviews, letters, journal entries, newspaper articles, character analyses, dialogue writing, college admission essays, and commercials. The goal is to make the difficult appear easy!

Whether you use these realistic classroom-tested activities for introduction, remediation, reinforcement, or enrichment, they will guide your students toward more effective writing. Many of the activities include riddles, hidden words and sayings, word-finds, and other devices that allow students to check their own answers. These activities will also help you to assess your students' progress.

So go ahead and make Mr. Faulkner proud by awakening the experience, observation, and imagination of your students. The benefits will be both theirs—and yours!

*Jack Umstatter*

# ABOUT UNIT 1

*Ready-to-Use Word Activities*, the first unit in the *Writing Skills Curriculum Library*, provides you with 90 creative, practical, and reproducible activities that encourage students to use words effectively and convincingly. You can choose the activity's implementation. Select pages for a unit's introduction or review as an individual, small group/cooperative learning, or entire-class activity. Some activities may be given as homework, research, or reinforcement assignments. They are also useful as discussion pieces concerning the construction, selection, and use of words. Some can be used for an entire period's lesson while others can be used to fill 10 or 15 minutes of class time. Some of the activities use magic squares, riddles, hidden words, sayings, word-finds, and other devices that allow students to check their own answers.

- Activities 1 through 19, "The Writer's Basics," form the foundation for the rest of the activities. The parts of speech, prefixes, spelling, words often confused, and word-building activities promote a greater knowledge of the basic tools necessary for effective writing.

- Activities 20 through 38, "A Way With Words," focus on vocabulary expansion. Activities that ask students to group words and see the relationships between words are found here. Additionally, word recognition and word selection activities foster keener interest in words.

- To "Write the Right Word," activities 39 through 55 help the student writers to select the best word for their needs. Seven word-specificity activities and six word-exactness activities reinforce the importance of clear and cogent expression.

- Activities 56 through 76 encourage students to implement their word knowledge. Selecting precise descriptions and using expressions skillfully will improve your students' ability to write with power.

- "A Potpourri of Puzzles," activities 77 through 99 are a puzzle lover's paradise. A combination of word-find, crossword, cryptology, and magic square puzzles will provide students with enjoyable and entertaining ways to improve their vocabulary and word awareness.

These activities will enhance student involvement and interest in words. My students have enjoyed them—and so will yours!

*Jack Umstatter*

# CONTENTS



## SECTION ONE
## THE WRITER'S BASICS

## SECTION TWO
# A WAY WITH WORDS



## SECTION THREE
# WRITING THE RIGHT WORD

## SECTION FOUR
## USING WORDS EFFECTIVELY

## SECTION FIVE
# A POTPOURRI OF PUZZLES

# TEACHER'S CORRECTION MARKS

| | |
|---|---|
| ab | abbreviation problem |
| agr | agreement problem |
| amb | ambiguous |
| awk | awkward expression or construction |
| cap | capitalize |
| case | error in case |
| cp | comma problem |
| cs | comma splice |
| d | inappropriate diction |
| det | details are needed |
| dm | dangling modifier |
| dn | double negative |
| frag | fragment |
| ital | italics or underline |
| lc | use lower case |
| mm | misplaced modifier |
| num | numbers problem |
| ^ | insert |
| ¶ | new paragraph needed |
| ‖ | faulty parallelism |
| , | insert comma |
| pass | misuse of passive voice |
| pr ref | pronoun reference problem |
| pun | punctuation needed or missing |
| reas | reasoning needs improvement |
| rep | unnecessary repetition |
| RO | run-on |
| shift | faulty tense shift |
| sp | incorrect spelling |
| thesis | improve the thesis |
| trans | improve the transition |
| TX | topic sentence needed (or improved) |
| U | usage problem |
| UW | unclear wording |
| V | variety needed |
| VAG | vague |
| VE | verb error |
| VT | verb tense problem |
| w | wordy |
| WC | better word choice |
| WM | word missing |
| WW | wrong word |

SECTION ONE

# THE WRITER'S BASICS

Name ____________________ Date __________ Period __________

# 1-1. FINDING FIVE

Each part of speech listed below is the answer to five different questions. Write the abbreviation (see the Key) for the word's part of speech in the space next to the word. The first one is done for you. After completing the last question, check to see that all five choices have been used five times each.

**Key:** adjective = adj; adverb = advb; conjunction = con; noun = n; verb = v

1. adj allergic
2. _____ although
3. _____ and
4. _____ appall
5. _____ baptize
6. _____ bolero
7. _____ ceremoniously
8. _____ coy
9. _____ diagnosis
10. _____ flunky
11. _____ for
12. _____ gracious
13. _____ heal
14. _____ lately
15. _____ manager
16. _____ or
17. _____ pacify
18. _____ pond
19. _____ reliable
20. _____ since
21. _____ soon
22. _____ strive
23. _____ trustful
24. _____ unduly
25. _____ willingly

Name ____________________ Date __________ Period __________

# 1-2. PARTS OF SPEECH

Each of the five different underlined words in the sentences below is a word that can be used as more than one part of speech. Identify the word's part of speech and write it in the appropriate space before the sentence. If your answers are correct, you will have found five nouns, five verbs, three adjectives, one adverb, and one preposition.

1. ______________ The tennis set was completed in one hour.
2. ______________ Can you set the table for us now?
3. ______________ Will it snow tomorrow?
4. ______________ Bill's snow shovel is in the garage.
5. ______________ We had more snow this year than we had last year.
6. ______________ Please down the ball once you catch it.
7. ______________ Hillary found the duck's down near the barn.
8. ______________ When the older person ran near him, the youngster fell down.
9. ______________ Let's walk down the hall now.
10. ______________ The Walters family placed a down payment on a new home.
11. ______________ Charles purchased a running machine to use for this exercise.
12. ______________ All the players were running around the track.
13. ______________ Running is a great conditioner.
14. ______________ Will he foot the bill?
15. ______________ Mom's foot hurt during the dance.

Name ______________________________ Date __________ Period __________

# 1-3. PARTS-OF-SPEECH VERSATILITY CHECK

Which words listed below are the most versatile? That is, which words can function as *several* parts of speech? Can any of them function as more than three parts of speech? These are just a few of the questions you will answer in this parts-of-speech versatility check.

On the appropriate lines, write the answers to the following ten questions. Each of the 20 words below is used only once. Use your dictionary if necessary.

| | | | | |
|---|---|---|---|---|
| academic | crow | learn | on | swell |
| catalog | economy | ministry | only | taboo |
| catastrophe | gorgeous | motor | ponder | truthfully |
| creed | into | note | prudent | vacuum |

1. Which words are nouns only?

______________________________

2. Which words are both nouns and verbs?

______________________________

3. Which words are verbs only?

______________________________

4. Which word is both a noun and an adjective?

______________________________

5. Which words are adjectives only?

______________________________

6. Which word is strictly an adverb?

______________________________

7. Which word is both an adjective and an adverb?

______________________________

8. Which word is only a preposition?

______________________________

9. Which four words can be three parts of speech?

______________________________

10. Which word is a noun, an adjective, an adverb, and a preposition?

______________________________

On the back of this sheet, use some of these words in sentences to show you know how they can function as various parts of speech.

Name ______________________________ Date __________ Period __________

# 1-4. PARTS-OF-SPEECH RACE

Using your dictionary, indicate how many different parts of speech each word can be. First write the specific parts of speech and then write the number of parts of speech in the indicated space. The first one is done for you. After completing each group, add up its total and then figure out which group has the highest total. Write the winning group's name in the appropriate space.

## *Group One*

1. fossil: ( 2 ) noun, adjective
2. raise: (___) ______________________
3. run: (___) ______________________
4. low: (___) ______________________
5. go: (___) ______________________

**Total** ______

## *Group Two*

1. ego: (___) ______________________
2. case: (___) ______________________
3. down: (___) ______________________
4. table: (___) ______________________
5. high: (___) ______________________

**Total** ______

## *Group Three*

1. salt: (___) ______________________
2. right: (___) ______________________
3. haul: (___) ______________________
4. cast: (___) ______________________
5. vent: (___) ______________________

**Total** ______

Which group has the highest total and wins the race? ______________________

Name ______________________________ Date __________ Period __________

# 1-5. A VARIETY OF WAYS

A skilled writer knows how to use words in a variety of ways. You are asked to do the same here. Use each word as suggested by the parts of speech following the word. Thus, you will use **break** as a *noun* and then as a *verb* in the first task. Use the word as it is; do not add prefixes or suffixes. Compare your answers with those of your classmates.

1. **break** (a) noun (b) verb

   (a) ______________________________

   (b) ______________________________

2. **grant** (a) noun (b) verb

   (a) ______________________________

   (b) ______________________________

3. **iron** (a) noun (b) verb (c) adjective

   (a) ______________________________

   (b) ______________________________

   (c) ______________________________

4. **light** (a) noun (b) verb (c) adjective (d) adverb

   (a) ______________________________

   (b) ______________________________

   (c) ______________________________

   (d) ______________________________

5. **nick** (a) noun (b) verb

   (a) ______________________________

   (b) ______________________________

6. **now** (a) adjective (b) adverb (c) conjunction

   (a) ______________________________

   (b) ______________________________

   (c) ______________________________

Name ______________________________ Date __________ Period __________

# 1-6. EVERYBODY HAS THREE!

Knowing your parts of speech will help you succeed in this activity. Each choice below—A, B, C, D, and E—will appear as the correct answer three times. Place the letter of the correct choice in the space next to the question's number. Then check that each choice has been used three times. Write a short sentence after each word that has an A, B or D answer to show that you know how it is used as that part of speech.

***The word functions as:***

A. Noun only

B. Verb only

C. Noun and Verb

D. Adjective only

E. None of the above

1. _____ reliable ______________________________
2. _____ invent ______________________________
3. _____ snow ______________________________
4. _____ govern ______________________________
5. _____ nevertheless ______________________________
6. _____ strengthen ______________________________
7. _____ bend ______________________________
8. _____ supposition ______________________________
9. _____ illusory ______________________________
10. _____ translucent ______________________________
11. _____ but ______________________________
12. _____ debtor ______________________________
13. _____ solidly ______________________________
14. _____ wonderment ______________________________
15. _____ place ______________________________

Name ______________________ Date __________ Period __________

# 1-7. GETTING TO KNOW THE WHOLE FAMILY

Knowing how a word can be changed to be used as other parts of speech will increase both your vocabulary and your ability to write effectively. In the spaces provided, write the correct form of the given word. Use only the present tense of the verb. The first set of words is done for you.

| *Noun* | *Verb* | *Adjective* | *Adverb* |
|---|---|---|---|
| 1. anger | anger | angry/angered | angrily |
| 2. barbarism | ___________ | ___________ | ___________ |
| 3. ___________ | ___________ | snow | ___________ |
| 4. ___________ | savor | savored/savory | ___________ |
| 5. report | ___________ | reported | ___________ |
| 6. preparedness | ___________ | ___________ | preparedly |
| 7. friend | ___________ | friendly | friendily |
| 8. reservation | ___________ | reserved | ___________ |
| 9. ___________ | freshen | ___________ | freshly |
| 10. ___________ | ___________ | ___________ | agreeably |

Name ______________________ Date __________ Period __________

# 1-8. PRONOUN PROBLEMS

These 20 sentences test your knowledge of pronoun usage. Underline the correct answer in each sentence and then write the number of letters in the correct answer on the line next to the question's number. If you have done all 20 correctly, you should score 32 for sentences 1–10 and the same, 32, for sentences 11–20. The first question is answered for you.

1. 2 The final match will be between you and (I, me).
2. ___ It is (her, she) at the door.
3. ___ The class officers asked (us, we) students for additional help.
4. ___ Each woman enjoyed (herself, themselves) at the reunion.
5. ___ Will you and (her, she) be able to go to the concert this weekend?
6. ___ The highest achievers were Stephanie and (her, she).
7. ___ Some of the papers (are, is) damaged.
8. ___ Did you want to go on the cruise with the Fullers and (us, we)?
9. ___ Either of the girls can tell you how (she, they) will travel to the studio.
10. ___ For (who, whom) shall I ask?

___ (Total letters)

11. ___ He sent mom and (I, me) several newspaper clippings.
12. ___ They are capable of doing the task by (theirselves, themselves).
13. ___ The man (who, whom) is our music teacher will be playing at Carnegie Hall this spring.
14. ___ Neither the pitcher nor the catcher was pleased with (his, their) performance.
15. ___ One of the sisters called (her, their) parents for a ride home.
16. ___ Anybody can reveal (his, their) deepest secret to that trusted individual.
17. ___ The photographer gave (us, we) members a discount.
18. ___ All of the meat (are, is) tainted.
19. ___ The wild animal bit both Mr. Price and (I, me).
20. ___ I am younger than (he, him).

___ (Total letters)

Name ______________________ Date __________ Period __________

# 1-9. CATCH 22

For each of the following 20 prefixes, write its value in the space next to the prefix. Thus, the number 8 will appear in the space next to the prefix "oct-." A number can be used more than once. Fractions are allowed. If you have answered the questions correctly, each group's prefix number total will be 22.

1. __8__ oct-
2. ____ ter-
3. ____ uni-
4. ____ quadr-
5. ____ hexa-

**Total** ____

11. ____ di-
12. ____ mono-
13. ____ sex-
14. ____ deca-
15. ____ tri-

**Total** ____

6. ____ hemi-
7. ____ sesqui-
8. ____ nona-
9. ____ tetr-
10. ____ sept-

**Total** ____

16. ____ demi-
17. ____ duodec-
18. ____ hepta-
19. ____ semi-
20. ____ duo-

**Total** ____

Name ______________________ Date __________ Period __________

# 1-10. IS IT INEQUAL OR UNEQUAL?

Prefixes are important tools for good writers. Knowing which prefixes to attach to which roots is important. Using a dictionary to clear up any confusion in this matter is always helpful. You may want to do just that in this activity.

For each prefix found beneath the 30 words in the box, write the five words that form their negative by using that particular prefix. Though some words may be able to be placed in more than one prefix group, decide which placement is best considering that each prefix must have five words as its answer. The first one is started for you.

| | | | | |
|---|---|---|---|---|
| avow | fair | legal | movable | regular |
| band | fertile | legible | passable | relevant |
| charge | fiction | legitimate | penitent | reparable |
| content | fortunate | licit | pertinent | resolute |
| equal | guarded | literate | porous | taxable |
| essential | hearten | mobilize | rational | usable |

1. **dis-** disavow ______________________

______________________

2. **il-** ______________________

______________________

3. **im-** ______________________

______________________

4. **ir-** ______________________

______________________

5. **non-** ______________________

______________________

6. **un-** ______________________

______________________

Name ________________________________ Date __________ Period __________

# 1-11. PREFIXES THAT NEGATE

The words **literate, mature,** and **responsible** are positive words that can be made into negative words by attaching prefixes to them. By adding the prefix **il-** to **literate,** the prefix **im-** to **mature,** and the prefix **ir-** to **responsible,** these three words now become negative words.

Match the 15 words in Column B with the Column A prefixes that make them negative. Write the appropriate letter from Column B in the space next to the correct number in Column A. If your answers are correct, you will have spelled out three words. Can you find them?

| *Column A* | *Column B* |
|---|---|
| 1. ___ ab- | A. prove |
| 2. ___ anti- | B. frequently |
| 3. ___ de- | C. functional |
| 4. ___ dis- | D. represent |
| 5. ___ dys- | E. nourished |
| 6. ___ ec- | F. communicate |
| 7. ___ ex- | G. modest |
| 8. ___ il- | H. normal |
| 9. ___ im- | I. climax |
| 10. ___ in- | J. frost |
| 11. ___ ir- | K. centric |
| 12. ___ mal- | L. rational |
| 13. ___ mis- | M. standard |
| 14. ___ non- | N. coordinated |
| 15. ___ un- | O. legal |

The three words found in the answer column are:

______________________________________________________________

Name ______________________ Date __________ Period __________

# 1-12. TOO MUCH OR TOO LITTLE?

Twenty misspelled words are found beneath the column entitled "Misspelled Word." Rewrite each correctly under the column "Correct Spelling." On the line under the column entitled "Letter," write the letter you either had to add or delete in order to spell the misspelled word correctly. If you have inserted the correct 20 letters, they will spell out, in order, a specific place. Write that place's name on the line at the bottom of this sheet.

| *Letter* | *Misspelled Word* | *Correct Spelling* |
|---|---|---|
| 1.____ | warant | ______________ |
| 2.____ | temperment | ______________ |
| 3.____ | colaborate | ______________ |
| 4.____ | bookkeper | ______________ |
| 5.____ | recept | ______________ |
| 6.____ | exagerate | ______________ |
| 7.____ | myrr | ______________ |
| 8.____ | inate | ______________ |
| 9.____ | phosphorus | ______________ |
| 10.____ | inferrior | ______________ |
| 11.____ | committment | ______________ |
| 12.____ | frigtening | ______________ |
| 13.____ | vaccuum | ______________ |
| 14.____ | filment | ______________ |
| 15.____ | prefered | ______________ |
| 16.____ | ballon | ______________ |
| 17.____ | folliage | ______________ |
| 18.____ | lesure | ______________ |
| 19.____ | mannual | ______________ |
| 20.____ | ardvark | ______________ |

The place is ______________________________________.

Name ______________________ Date __________ Period __________

# 1-13. SPELLING YOUR WAY TO THE MOVIE'S TITLE

One word in each 3-word group is spelled incorrectly. Spell that word correctly in the appropriate space in Column D. Then write that word's first letter on the line at the bottom of this sheet. Unscramble these 16 letters to form the name of a 4-word movie title beginning with the letter F.

| | *Column A* | *Column B* | *Column C* | *Column D* |
|---|---|---|---|---|
| 1. | similar | familar | symmetry | ______________ |
| 2. | psychology | trustworthy | eligable | ______________ |
| 3. | swelter | despare | intrigue | ______________ |
| 4. | hilarous | mechanical | confusing | ______________ |
| 5. | latitude | yesterday | tomorow | ______________ |
| 6. | special | harrass | terrible | ______________ |
| 7. | esteam | modify | fluctuate | ______________ |
| 8. | repetition | forfiet | difference | ______________ |
| 9. | embarrass | portable | begginning | ______________ |
| 10. | emphasize | reccommend | remember | ______________ |
| 11. | ocurred | rehearsal | questionable | ______________ |
| 12. | procession | excellant | eulogy | ______________ |
| 13. | phantom | refuseal | benefited | ______________ |
| 14. | marginal | existence | temperment | ______________ |
| 15. | approach | ilegal | reception | ______________ |
| 16. | aproval | maneuver | beautiful | ______________ |

Write the 16 letters here: ______________________________________

The 4-word movie title is: ______________________________________

Name ______________________ Date __________ Period __________

# 1-14. SPELLING IN PARTS

Connect the three parts of the ten spelling words in each group by joining one part from Column A, one part from Column B, and one part from Column C. Place the correctly spelled word on the blank line next to Column A. The word should start with the letter combination found in Column A. Each part is used only once. All parts will be used. The first one is done for you.

## *Group One*

| *Correctly Spelled Word* | *Column A* | *Column B* | *Column C* |
|---|---|---|---|
| 1. blinding | bli | der | city |
| 2. ______________ | chal | en | ge |
| 3. ______________ | circum | end | ical |
| 4. ______________ | fri | er | igate |
| 5. ______________ | grat | it | ing |
| 6. ______________ | num | len | ony |
| 7. ______________ | off | nav | ous |
| 8. ______________ | sim | nd | ship |
| 9. ______________ | sym | ph | sive |
| 10. ______________ | thun | pli | ude |

## *Group Two*

| *Correctly Spelled Word* | *Column A* | *Column B* | *Column C* |
|---|---|---|---|
| 1. ______________ | com | ck | al |
| 2. ______________ | eff | dard | ful |
| 3. ______________ | horr | der | ical |
| 4. ______________ | il | ect | it |
| 5. ______________ | mys | end | ively |
| 6. ______________ | myth | lic | ized |
| 7. ______________ | per | olog | ment |
| 8. ______________ | stan | ple | ness |
| 9. ______________ | thi | sua | ous |
| 10. ______________ | won | tic | sive |

Name ______________________________ Date __________ Period __________

# 1-15. MAKING THE UNCLEAR CLEAR

Show your knowledge of words that sound the same but are spelled differently by writing the correct word in each blank. The initial letter of each word is given to help you recognize the word. Additionally, the first sentence is already done for you.

1. By the time we were all ready to go, the other group had already left the parking lot.
2. What a____________ would you a____________ us to take?
3. It is always wise to use really old c____________ as c____________ for cleaning.
4. Four hours quickly p____________ when the reunion members talked about the p____________.
5. Can you h____________ us from h____________?
6. W____________ or not the w____________ cooperates with us will have a big influence on our plans tomorrow.
7. After the operation, Grandpa was too w____________ to put in a full w____________ of work.
8. Y____________ going to miss y____________ bus if you don't hurry.
9. It was not t____________ decision to go over t____________, but t____________ still going anyway.
10. Regina wanted you t__________ go t__________.
11. What p____________ of discipline does the new school's p____________ follow?
12. In the home economics c____________ you will be taught how to wash c____________ fabrics.
13. Tim had to a____________ his wedding tuxedo so he would look handsome on the a____________.
14. The p____________ landed safely on the p____________.
15. Our substitute teacher was q____________ happy that we were so q____________.

Name ______________________ Date __________ Period __________

# 1-16. ONE OF THEM

Each of the words within the parentheses is often confused with the other words in the group. Noting how these words differ from each other, circle the most appropriate choice in each sentence. Compare your answers with those of your classmates and be prepared to explain your choices. Dictionaries are suggested!

1. Joe (recited, rendered, said, vowed) he would never use his brother's clothes without his permission.
2. Having a CD player in a movie set in the 1800s is an example of a(n) (anachronism, obsoleteness, redundancy).
3. The importer had to pay the (lien, mortgage, tariff) on the incoming goods.
4. Union and management reached a(n) (draw, impasse, tie) in their attempts to come to an agreement.
5. At sixty years old, Helen was a (greenie, novice, starter) at tennis.
6. After fifteen hours of deliberation, the jury reached a (resolution, resolve, verdict).
7. The students (agreed, complied, conformed) with the teacher's wishes and wrote their reports again.
8. The local government passed a(n) (law, ordinance, regulation) restricting the sale of the land near the highway.
9. Several opera fans complained to the (conductor, impresario, impressionist) about the air conditioner in the opera house.
10. The incumbent needed to pay more attention to the (constituents, electorates, insurgents) who had voted her into office.
11. The (talented, smart, witty) child played difficult musical compositions and the audience showed much appreciation.
12. The performer was hurt by the (disparaging, distraught, engaging) remarks of the newspaper's music critic.
13. The (ominous, reckless, vigilant) clouds were enough warning to those at the picnic to seek shelter.
14. When the singer (fostered, retorted, snubbed) us after the concert, we left very unhappily.
15. The surgeon's (incision, indentation, slash) could not have been cleaner.

Name ______________________ Date __________ Period __________

# 1-17. AWARDS

These 19 questions feature pairs of words that are often confused with each other. Circle the correct choice for each question and then write the choice's letter in the space after the question's number. Write the answer letters in consecutive order on the line at the bottom of this sheet. If you have answered all the questions correctly, you will understand the sense behind this activity's title.

1. _______ Which is the bundle? (O) bale (P) bail
2. _______ Which is the study of celestial bodies? (R) astrology (S) astronomy
3. _______ Which is the path? (C) route (D) rout
4. _______ Which means lazy? (A) indolent (B) idle
5. _______ Which is correct? (R) a vendetta is part of a feud (S) a feud is part of a vendetta
6. _______ Which is the bottom? (E) nadir (F) zenith
7. _______ Which is more hurtful to the recipient? (M) to chafe (B) to chaff
8. _______ Which word is more specific? (L) regal (M) royal
9. _______ Which is worse? (X) calamity (Y) catastrophe
10. _______ Which is used for flying? (T) plane (U) plain
11. _______ Which is stronger? (O) doubtful (P) dubious
12. _______ Which means to be superior to another? (M) succinct (N) surpass
13. _______ Which is the woman engaged to be married? (X) fiancé (7) fiancee
14. _______ Which is the building? (G) capitol (H) capital
15. _______ Which is your hobby? (Q) vocation (R) avocation
16. _______ Who studies weather? (A) meteorologist (B) metrologist
17. _______ Which is spread without human contact? (M) infectious (N) contagious
18. _______ Which is the rule? (L) principal (M) principle
19. _______ Which implies a feeling of worry? (X) eager (Y) anxious

Letters: ______________________________________

Name ________________________ Date __________ Period __________

# 1-18. WHAT'S THE DIFFERENCE?

What is the difference when a person's interest is *avid* and when it is *fanatical?* Is it wiser to be *daring* or *reckless?* Is there a difference? Using the dictionary, show the difference between the words in these 15 pairs of closely related words by writing the definitions on the appropriate line. Discuss your answers and ideas with your classmates.

1. avid: ______________________________
   fanatical: ______________________________
2. concerned: ______________________________
   officious: ______________________________
3. continual: ______________________________
   continuous: ______________________________
4. credible: ______________________________
   credulous: ______________________________
5. curt: ______________________________
   terse: ______________________________
6. daring: ______________________________
   reckless: ______________________________
7. disinterested: ______________________________
   indifferent: ______________________________
8. famous: ______________________________
   infamous: ______________________________
9. firm: ______________________________
   stubborn: ______________________________
10. hound: ______________________________
    pursue: ______________________________
11. immoral: ______________________________
    amoral: ______________________________
12. sarcastic: ______________________________
    sardonic: ______________________________
13. stroll: ______________________________
    strut: ______________________________
14. willfully: ______________________________
    willingly: ______________________________
15. wise: ______________________________
    pedantic: ______________________________

Name ______________________________ Date __________ Period __________

# 1-19. FORMING THE WORDS

Your ability to form words will come in handy here. Fifteen words have been divided into three parts. Using one part from each of the three columns (A, B, and C), write the word that begins with the letters in Column A on the line next to that column. Thus, if you use **com** from Column A, **pre** from Column B, and **hend** from Column C, you will form the word **comprehend.** Write that word on the first blank line and then continue to form 14 more words. Remember that each combination of letters can only be used once.

| *Word* | *Column A* | *Column B* | *Column C* |
|---|---|---|---|
| ____________ | com | advert | able |
| ____________ | crit | er | al |
| ____________ | demo | gene | an |
| ____________ | dis | graph | ate |
| ____________ | equi | is | ed |
| ____________ | homo | iter | ent |
| ____________ | im | mor | hend |
| ____________ | in | morph | ic |
| ____________ | ir | par | ics |
| ____________ | meta | passion | ion |
| ____________ | para | pre | ious |
| ____________ | part | psycho | ity |
| ____________ | pre | revoc | logy |
| ____________ | re | tent | osis |
| ____________ | sopho | voc | ous |

SECTION TWO

# A WAY WITH WORDS

Name ______________________________ Date __________ Period __________

# 1-20. POSITIVE AND NEGATIVE ADJECTIVES

Adjectives are invaluable tools for a writer. They allow the reader to get a fuller look at a person, place, thing, or idea. A writer who merely says it is a sweater does not help the reader so much as the writer who says the sweater is green and woolen. Thus, adjectives are important for both the writer and the reader.

All the adjectives in Column A have positive associations while those adjectives in Column B have negative associations. Some adjectives have been provided for you. In each blank write an appropriate adjective that begins with the letter in Column A. Share your answers with your classmates.

| *Starting letter* | *Column A (positive)* | *Column B (negative)* |
|---|---|---|
| a | agile | ____________ |
| b | ____________ | bland |
| c | caring | ____________ |
| d | diligent | ____________ |
| e | elegant | ____________ |
| f | friendly | ____________ |
| g | ____________ | ghastly |
| h | ____________ | horrible |
| i | ____________ | immature |
| j | jovial | ____________ |
| k | kind | ____________ |
| l | ____________ | lonely |
| m | ____________ | mean |
| n | nimble | ____________ |
| o | objective | ____________ |
| p | ____________ | poor |
| q | quaint | ____________ |
| r | ____________ | rancid |
| s | sensible | ____________ |
| t | ____________ | terrible |
| u | ____________ | uninspired |
| v | ____________ | violent |
| w | wonderful | ____________ |
| y | youthful | ____________ |
| z | zesty | ____________ |

Name ______________________ Date __________ Period __________

# 1-21. SENSATIONAL WORDS

These 20 words are adjectives that are associated with our five senses. Unscramble them and write the correct spelling in the appropriate spaces. Then, using the circled letters, write those 20 letters (in consecutive order) on the appropriate line at the bottom of this sheet. These letters will form four words whose definitions are given.

1. ◯ _ _ _ _ _ ibettr
2. ◯ _ _ _ _ erkey
3. _ _ ◯ _ _ psciy
4. _ _ _ _ _ _ ◯ rbtelti
5. ◯ _ _ _ _ oyfgg
6. _ _ _ _ ◯ lnbda
7. _ _ _ ◯ _ _ rcayem
8. _ _ _ ◯ _ tyats
9. _ _ _ ◯ _ _ _ _ kelurwam
10. ◯ _ _ _ ttra
11. ◯ _ _ _ radi
12. _ ◯ _ _ lyio
13. _ _ ◯ _ ylgu
14. ◯ _ _ yrd
15. _ _ ◯ _ _ _ pryett
16. _ _ _ ◯ _ _ _ _ _ deaingfen
17. _ ◯ _ tew
18. _ _ _ _ _ _ _ ◯ artcoima
19. _ ◯ _ _ _ iyhtc
20. _ _ ◯ _ _ styru

__________________ (#1–5) synonym for short; antonym for long

__________________ (#6–9) a fruit; January 4 is one; to go out with

__________________ (#10–13) the end of a plane

__________________ (#14–20) deficiencies; shortcomings; imperfections

Name ______________________________ Date __________ Period __________

# 1-22. MAKING SENSE OF ANALOGIES

On the line after each analogy, write the relationship of the two words. Then on the other side of this sheet, write a similar analogy for each of these 25 analogies. Discuss your answers with your classmates.

1. puzzle : cryptic ______________________________
2. idle : work ______________________________
3. plunder : ransack ______________________________
4. trivial : doodad ______________________________
5. veracity : duplicity ______________________________
6. inflammable : flammable ______________________________
7. awkward : lithe ______________________________
8. despot : tyrant ______________________________
9. vice : virtue ______________________________
10. bisect : cut ______________________________
11. postscript : after ______________________________
12. counsel : advice ______________________________
13. deluge : drought ______________________________
14. defer : delay ______________________________
15. ultra- : beyond ______________________________
16. inter- : between ______________________________
17. intro- : outside ______________________________
18. dilemma : easy ______________________________
19. tolerant : disrespectful ______________________________
20. friction : smoothness ______________________________
21. Venus : ugliness ______________________________
22. avid : eager ______________________________
23. green : envy ______________________________
24. inferior : superior ______________________________
25. arson : fire ______________________________

Name ______________________ Date __________ Period __________

# 1-23. KNOCKING DOWN THOSE ANALOGIES!

If you answer each of these analogies correctly and place the answer's corresponding letter in the space before the analogy, you will spell two words that are associated with the title. Write those two words at the bottom of this sheet.

1. ____ **tooth : comb** (A) plank : wood (B) sofa : cushion (C) inning : baseball game
2. ____ **fervent : impassioned** (M) walk : run (N) light : filament (O) diffident : shy
3. ____ **ante- : before** (L) morph- : date (M) poly- : many (N) graph- : read
4. ____ **aria : opera** (P) soliloquy : drama (Q) autumn : leaves (R) television : radio
5. ____ **sadist : others** (A) masochist : self (B) baton : self (C) ruler : centimeter
6. ____ **instigate : end** (Q) plow : tool (R) gigantic : dwarfish (S) titular : name
7. ____ **vascular : veins** (G) cardiologist : eyes (H) dental : nose (I) dermatological : skin
8. ____ **epigram : long** (R) monologue : alone (S) epic : brief (T) terse : short
9. ____ **thespian : stage** (M) teacher : field (N) baseball player : locker room (O) orator : platform
10. ____ **dank : wet** (M) pithy : long (N) arid : dry (O) chalk : wood
11. ____ **epee : fencer** (S) baton : conductor (T) glove : golfer (U) mitt : batter
12. ____ **draft : essay** (A) proof : photographer (B) product : drawing (C) finale : play
13. ____ **snake : slough** (M) sheep : shear (N) bird : molt (O) barber : shave
14. ____ **architect : builder** (A) designer : suit (B) hod : bricks (C) electrician : meter
15. ____ **pinnacle : top** (K) modicum : wealth (L) nadir : bottom (M) high : airplane
16. ____ **bracelet : jewelry** (N) watch : time (O) carriage : vehicle (P) necklace : neck
17. ____ **edge : paper** (G) shoulder : road (H) water : beach (I) molehill : mountain
18. ____ **run : sprint** (G) rain : trickle (H) walk : (I) drive : speed
19. ____ **moon : wax** (C) hurt : recuperate (D) tide : ebb (E) population : expand
20. ____ **lawyer : counsel** (S) psychiatrist : therapy (T) driver : route (U) enemy : solution

The two words spelled are ______________________________________________.

Name ______________________________ Date __________ Period __________

# 1-24. DOUBLING THE SIZE

Twenty-four adjectives dealing with size are found below. Eight words are adjectives meaning *small* and 16 words are adjectives meaning *large*. Write each word in its appropriate column.

| | | |
|---|---|---|
| capacious | gigantic | minute |
| colossal | huge | narrow |
| confined | immense | perpetual |
| cramped | infinite | prodigious |
| diminutive | mammoth | puny |
| elephantine | massive | roomy |
| eternal | measureless | towering |
| extensive | minuscule | trivial |

| ***Small*** | ***Large*** | |
|---|---|---|
| ______________ | ______________ | ______________ |
| ______________ | ______________ | ______________ |
| ______________ | ______________ | ______________ |
| ______________ | ______________ | ______________ |
| ______________ | ______________ | ______________ |
| ______________ | ______________ | ______________ |
| ______________ | ______________ | ______________ |
| ______________ | ______________ | ______________ |

Name ______________________ Date __________ Period __________

# 1-25. TRIPLE THREAT

Ten different words, each having three definitions, are the answers to the following questions. The answer's first letter appears after the word's third definition.

1. ______________ part of a house; part of a bowling game; part of a film **(F)**
2. ______________ part of a journey; part of a body; part of a triangle **(L)**
3. ______________ part of the body; part of a city; part of a vegetable **(H)**
4. ______________ part of a tennis match; part of a square dance; part of a math answer **(S)**
5. ______________ part of a comb; part of a saw; part of a fork **(T)**
6. ______________ part of a book; part of a deed; part of a name **(T)**
7. ______________ part of a glass; part of an inning; part of a crate **(B)**
8. ______________ part of a clock; part of a card; part of a domino **(F)**
9. ______________ part of a river; part of a glass; part of a cave **(M)**
10. ______________ part of a process; part of a ladder; part of a supply pipe **(S)**

On the back of this sheet, make up five examples similar to the ones above. Share your examples with your classmates.

Name ______________________ Date __________ Period __________

# 1-26. WORDS WITH MULTIPLE MEANINGS

In a typical college dictionary, the word **run** has over 100 meanings! Each word below has many different meanings. Match the words with their correct meanings by writing the correct answer in the appropriate space. A word may be used more than once.

**act bed drive fall run set**

1. ______________________ number of couples needed for a square dance
2. ______________________ large-scale military offensive
3. ______________________ to be killed in battle
4. ______________________ unit of tennis
5. ______________________ division of a wrestling match
6. ______________________ unit of a play
7. ______________________ bottom of a river
8. ______________________ continuous series
9. ______________________ to operate a motor vehicle
10. ______________________ law
11. ______________________ to serve as a substitute for
12. ______________________ flat surface used as a foundation
13. ______________________ to flow off or drain
14. ______________________ topple
15. ______________________ computer component
16. ______________________ to fix a time for
17. ______________________ migration of fish
18. ______________________ determined
19. ______________________ to appear to be
20. ______________________ plot of soil where plants are raised

Name ______________________ Date __________ Period __________

# 1-27. COME AND JOIN US

Each group of words will be complete when you correctly fill in one of the 15 words from the Word Bank. In the space following each question's number, write the synonym that completes that group.

***Word Bank***

| | | | | |
|---|---|---|---|---|
| augment | recoup | spite | tarry | valorous |
| employment | rummage | stubborn | tumult | vogue |
| fracture | shrouded | sustain | utility | wax |

1. ______________ pigheaded mulish obstinate
2. ______________ ransack hunt search
3. ______________ brave lionhearted heroic
4. ______________ smash crash splinter
5. ______________ loiter remain linger
6. ______________ recover retrieve regain
7. ______________ enlarge supplement increase
8. ______________ fashion mode look
9. ______________ labor work job
10. ______________ uproar discord turmoil
11. ______________ value worth merit
12. ______________ grow increase expand
13. ______________ hidden veiled masked
14. ______________ jealousy resentment grudge
15. ______________ nurture feed maintain

Name ______________________ Date __________ Period __________

# 1-28. GROUPING THE ACTIONS TOGETHER

The words in bold capital letters are the six group headings. Each group has been assigned a number. Next to each of the 30 words listed below the headings, write the appropriate group's number. When you have finished, each group should have five words.

**(1) BAN (2) CLASH (3) HUG (4) LEAD (5) STOP (6) THINK**

| | | |
|---|---|---|
| ____ bar | ____ consider | ____ meditate |
| ____ battle | ____ contend | ____ outlaw |
| ____ cease | ____ desist | ____ ponder |
| ____ clasp | ____ discontinue | ____ preclude |
| ____ clench | ____ dispute | ____ prohibit |
| ____ clutch | ____ embrace | ____ restrain |
| ____ command | ____ escort | ____ squeeze |
| ____ conceive | ____ forbid | ____ struggle |
| ____ conduct | ____ guide | ____ terminate |
| ____ conflict | ____ imagine | ____ usher |

Name ______________________________ Date __________ Period __________

# 1-29. HAPPY? SAD? CONFUSED?

Twenty-one words that deal with the concepts of happiness, sadness, and confusion are found below. Write these words in their appropriate columns. After you and your classmates have agreed upon the seven correct answers for each group, discuss how the words within each group differ from one another.

| | | | |
|---|---|---|---|
| baffled | depressed | gratified | satisfied |
| bewildered | disheartened | heartbroken | stupefied |
| crushed | downcast | mystified | thrilled |
| dejected | elated | perplexed | tickled |
| delighted | flustered | pleased | uncertain |
| | | | unhappy |

| *Happy* | *Sad* | *Confused* |
|---|---|---|
| ____________ | ____________ | ____________ |
| ____________ | ____________ | ____________ |
| ____________ | ____________ | ____________ |
| ____________ | ____________ | ____________ |
| ____________ | ____________ | ____________ |
| ____________ | ____________ | ____________ |
| ____________ | ____________ | ____________ |

Name ______________________________ Date __________ Period __________

# 1-30. DICTIONARY DASH

Circle the correct answer for each question. Then write the answer's letter in the space next to the question's number. If your answers are correct, there are 9 with the letter A and 11 with the letter B. If necessary, use a dictionary.

1. ___ Which two are the same? **(A)** 'til and 'till **(B)** till and until
2. ___ Which is associated with swelling? **(A)** turbid **(B)** turgid
3. ___ Is the political organization called a **(A)** bloc or a **(B)** block?
4. ___ Which is larger—a **(A)** cave or a **(B)** cavern?
5. ___ If one moves in a sneaky way, does that person **(A)** skulk or **(B)** sulk?
6. ___ Which of these words has a positive meaning? **(A)** prolific **(B)** profligate
7. ___ Which means to lessen in quality? **(A)** detract **(B)** distract
8. ___ Which doctor works *specifically* with a person's feet? **(A)** podiatrist **(B)** pediatrician
9. ___ Are the words *selfish* and *selfless* synonyms? **(A)** Yes **(B)** No
10. ___ The noun form of the adjective *candid* is **(A)** candidness **(B)** candor.
11. ___ The plural of the word *ox* is **(A)** oxen **(B)** oxis.
12. ___ The word *queue* has **(A)** one **(B)** two syllables.
13. ___ A female hero is called a **(A)** heroess **(B)** heroine.
14. ___ The plural form of father-in-law is **(A)** fathers'-in-law **(B)** fathers-in-law.
15. ___ Which is the combat troop? **(A)** calvary **(B)** cavalry
16. ___ Which person dabbles in different areas? **(A)** connoisseur **(B)** dilettante
17. ___ Which is a synonym for wickedness? **(A)** inequity **(B)** iniquity
18. ___ How many syllables are in the word *erudite?* **(A)** three **(B)** four
19. ___ An epaulet is on the **(A)** shoulder **(B)** sleeve of a military uniform.
20. ___ Which expression means "to attack"? **(A)** hand over fist **(B)** lay hands on

Name ______________________ Date __________ Period __________

# 1-31. PEOPLE'S CHARACTERISTICS

Writers can use many different words to characterize a person as either good or bad. These words lend shades of meaning to that character's personality. By expanding your vocabulary, you improve your ability to describe a character's personality more precisely. In this way, you will become a more efficient writer.

Twenty-six words used by writers to describe their characters are listed below. Write the letter **P** next to the words that have *positive* associations and the letter **N** next to those words that have *negative* associations. If your answers are correct, you will have found 13 positives and 13 negatives.

| | | | |
|---|---|---|---|
| __ acerbic | __ cold-blooded | __ diplomatic | __ persevering |
| __ amiable | __ congenial | __ discreet | __ repulsive |
| __ benevolent | __ credible | __ empathetic | __ sturdy |
| __ brash | __ credulous | __ gallant | __ timorous |
| __ brutish | __ deceptive | __ gracious | __ willful |
| __ callous | __ deficient | __ honorable | |
| __ civil | __ despondent | __ impudent | |

Name ______________________ Date __________ Period __________

# 1-32. LANGUAGE CONCISENESS

Using precise language is important for writers. Why say "the long, yellow motor vehicle that transports children to school" when you can say "the school bus"? Definitions of objects or places are listed below. Write the defined word on the line next to the number. The number of letters in the answer appears after the definition.

1. ______________ a container with a wick for burning oil **(4)**
2. ______________ the country directly north of the United States **(6)**
3. ______________ a smooth surface that reflects the images of objects **(6)**
4. ______________ the self-luminous central star of the solar system **(3)**
5. ______________ the flap under the laces or strap of a shoe **(6)**
6. ______________ a large printed card or sheet of paper used to advertise or publicize something **(6)**
7. ______________ a vehicle mounted on runners for use on snow or ice **(4)**
8. ______________ a large, aquatic mammal that is not a porpoise or a dolphin **(5)**
9. ______________ vaporous matter arising from something that is burning **(5)**
10. ______________ the joint connecting the arm or forelimb with the body **(8)**
11. ______________ a mass of smoke, dust, or steam **(5)**
12. ______________ a kind of table sometimes equipped with drawers and a flat or sloping top for writing or drawing **(4)**
13. ______________ a large piece of cloth used for warmth **(7)**
14. ______________ chart of the zodiacal signs and the position of the planets **(9)**
15. ______________ a small, slender piece of steel with a sharp point at one end and a hole for thread at the other **(6)**
16. ______________ a natural raised part of the Earth's surface, larger than a hill **(8)**
17. ______________ a film; a showing of a film, as in a theater **(5)**
18. ______________ a liquid or semisolid substance used on the body to prevent or destroy undesired odors **(9)**
19. ______________ a place of refuge or a protected inlet **(6)**
20. ______________ something set up to keep alive the memory of a person or event, as a tablet, statue, or pillar **(8)**

Name ______________________ Date __________ Period __________

# 1-33. DIS ME!

Twenty words beginning with the prefix "dis-" are found in Column A. Twenty definitions with their corresponding letters (within the parentheses) are found in Column B. Match the Column A words with their Column B definitions and write the corresponding three-letter combination on the line next to the question's number. If you answer all 20 questions correctly, you will spell the names of six Canadian cities and one Canadian province. Write those seven names at the bottom of this sheet.

| *Column A* | *Column B* |
|---|---|
| 1. _____ disbar | recognize the difference between (BEC) |
| 2. _____ discriminate | to upset (BIA) |
| 3. _____ discuss | well defined (BRI) |
| 4. _____ disdain | to reject with aloof contempt (COU) |
| 5. _____ disgust | rumple (HAL) |
| 6. _____ dishevel | to divide and give out in shares (HCO) |
| 7. _____ dismal | depressing (IFA) |
| 8. _____ dismay | to break up and scatter (LED) |
| 9. _____ disparage | discredit (LGA) |
| 10. _____ display | a geographical or political division (LUM) |
| 11. _____ dispute | far away (MON) |
| 12. _____ disrupt | to quarrel (ONT) |
| 13. _____ dissipate | deprive of the right to practice law (QUE) |
| 14. _____ distant | to disturb (REA) |
| 15. _____ distill | exhibit (RYM) |
| 16. _____ distinct | to cause sorrow or misery (TIS) |
| 17. _____ distress | to purify or refine (TON) |
| 18. _____ distribute | to talk or write about (VAN) |
| 19. _____ district | be sickening (VER) |
| 20. _____ disturb | fill with apprehension (XCA) |

The six Canadian cities are ______________________________________________.

The Canadian province is ______________________________________________.

Name ______________________ Date __________ Period __________

# 1-34. IDENTIFYING AND SPELLING THE SYNONYMS

Good writers have command over vocabulary. They can express themselves more clearly because they know words and how to use them. This activity will help you to assess both your synonym and spelling skills. Fill in the missing letters of the synonyms for each of the six words in bold letters.

1. **cut** (a) g __ __ h; (b) __ __ __ s h; (c) l __ n __ __; (d) __ l __ __; (e) __ __ __ e r

2. **emblem** (a) __ y m __ __ __; (b) i __ __ __ g __ i a; (c) __ __ k __ n; (d) b __ __ g __; (e) t o __ __ m

3. **gather** (a) c __ __ __ e c __; (b) __ c c __ __ __ l a __ e; (c) p __ __ e; (d) a __ __ s __; (e) g l __ __ __

4. **make** (a) f a b __ __ __ __ __ e; (b) m a __ __ __ __ c t __ r e; (c) m __ __ t; (d) p r __ __ __ c e; (e) c __ __ s t __ __ c t

5. **obscure** (a) v __ __ __ e; (b) u n c __ __ __ __; (c) c r __ __ __ i c; (d) i n d __ __ __ __ i t e; (e) u n c e __ __ __ __ __

6. **prudence** (a) __ a u t __ __ n; (b) c a __ __; (c) __ __ n s e; (d) s a g __ __ __ __ __; (e) e c __ __ __ m y

Name ______________________ Date __________ Period __________

# 1-35. IDENTIFYING AND SPELLING THE ANTONYMS

Your vocabulary and spelling skills will assist you in this antonym activity. Each word in bold is followed by 5 of its antonyms. Fill in the missing letters of these antonyms. How many of these 25 antonyms can you identify—and spell correctly?

1. **divide** (a) j ___ ___ n; (b) u n ___ ___ ___; (c) ___ i n k; (d) c ___ ___ ___ e c ___;
(e) m ___ ___ g ___

2. **purge** (a) s ___ ___ l; (b) ___ t a i ___; (c) d e ___ ___ ___ e; (d) p ___ ___ ___ u t ___;
(e) s ___ ___ ___ y

3. **aromatic** (a) r e ___ ___ y; (b) r ___ n k; (c) r ___ ___ c i ___; (d) s ___ ___ l l y;
(e) s ___ ___ r

4. **trustworthy** (a) i r r ___ ___ p o n ___ ___ ___ ___ ___; (b) d i s h ___ ___ ___ ___ t;
(c) d o ___ ___ ___ f u l; (d) q u ___ s ___ ___ o n a ___ ___ ___;
(e) i m p e ___ ___ ___ a b l e

5. **worsen** (a) i ___ p ___ o v ___; (b) b ___ ___ ___ e r; (c) ___ m e ___ ___;
(d) ___ e p ___ ___ r; (e) r e h ___ ___ ___ ___ i ___ a t e

Name ______________________________ Date __________ Period __________

# 1-36. WORD WEALTH

Here is your chance to show your word wealth. Several letters are given to start a word. Read the criterion that follows the question's number. Then complete the words in that group by adding the necessary letters. Your answers may vary from those of your classmates. Compare!

1. **All must be verbs.** as__________; per__________; te__________; yo__________; acq__________; gro__________
2. **All must be adjectives.** br__________; inq__________; ma__________; dem__________; fli__________; lo__________
3. **All must be things (no proper names).** ra__________; gri__________; ir__________ fo__________; pre__________; hi__________
4. **All must be adverbs.** pat__________; mea__________; de__________; sto__________; ea__________; jo__________
5. **All must be pronouns.** yo__________; he__________; mi__________; ou__________; the__________; i__________
6. **All must be occupations.** me__________; do__________; te__________; p__________; ar__________; an__________
7. **All must be negative adjectives.** de__________; anti__________; mal__________; un__________; il__________; dre__________
8. **All must be positive adjectives.** gr__________; be__________; fa__________; wo__________; lu__________; g__________

Name ______________________ Date __________ Period __________

# 1-37. FILLING IN THOSE ADVERBS

Good writers use effective adverbs to describe their characters' actions. Show your adverb and vocabulary versatility by filling in the missing letters of the following 20 sets of adverbs. There can be several different answers for each adverb. The first set of adverbs is already done for you.

1. ar<u>tistical</u>ly  art<u>ful</u>ly
2. be__________ly  be__________ly
3. br__________ly  br__________ly
4. can__________ly  can__________ly
5. el__________ly  el__________ly
6. fl__________ly  fl__________ly
7. gr__________ly  gr__________ly
8. hand__________ly  hand__________ly
9. man__________ly  man__________ly
10. par__________ly  par__________ly
11. pe__________ly  pe__________ly
12. qu__________ly  qu__________ly
13. re__________ly  re__________ly
14. sp__________ly  sp__________ly
15. su__________ly  su__________ly
16. te__________ly  te__________ly
17. th__________ly  th__________ly
18. un__________ly  un__________ly
19. vi__________ly  vi__________ly
20. wh__________ly  wh__________ly

Name ______________________ Date __________ Period __________

# 1-38. MYTHOLOGICAL NAMES, DERIVATIONS, AND CURRENT MEANINGS

Mythological allusions are often used by writers. Whatever the author's purpose in citing the mythological name, the reader is able to understand the reading better if he or she knows the mythological reference. Many of these names also have interesting origins.

Match the three columns by placing the two letters, one from Column B and one from Column C, on the line next to the appropriate number in Column A. If necessary, use your dictionary to find these meanings and derivations.

### *Column A (Word)*

1. _____ bacchanal
2. _____ cereal
3. _____ cupidity
4. _____ herculean
5. _____ martial
6. _____ mentor
7. _____ mercurial
8. _____ mnemonic
9. _____ narcissistic
10. _____ stygian
11. _____ tantalize
12. _____ titanic

### *Column B (Meaning)*

A. dark; gloomy
B. memory device
C. grains
D. great size
E. greed
F. self-love
G. to tease with an object and then withdraw it
H. very powerful
I. volatile; changeable
J. warlike
K. wild, drunken party
L. wise, loyal advisor

### *Column C (Derivation)*

M. beautiful Greek youth
N. counselor of Telemachus, son of Odysseus
O. mythological race of giants
P. river in Hades
Q. Roman god of love
R. Roman god of strength
S. Roman god of war
T. Roman god of wine
U. Roman goddess of grains and harvest
V. Roman messenger god
W. son of Zeus
X. wife of Zeus and parent of the nine Muses

SECTION THREE

# WRITING THE RIGHT WORD

Name ______________________ Date __________ Period __________

# 1-39. BE MORE SPECIFIC

Match each word in the *General* column with its more specific counterpart in the *More Specific* column. Write the correct letter next to its corresponding number. If you answer all the questions correctly, you will spell a synonym each for happy, a sound, a type of hairstyle, and a man's first name. Write those four words at the appropriate places at the bottom of this sheet.

| *General* | *More Specific* |
|---|---|
| 1. _____ animal | A. podiatrist |
| 2. _____ automobile | B. happiness |
| 3. _____ cloud | C. sofa |
| 4. _____ doctor | D. lemonade |
| 5. _____ drink | E. novel |
| 6. _____ emotion | F. continent |
| 7. _____ exercise | G. sedan |
| 8. _____ farming tool | H. aria |
| 9. _____ furniture | I. plow |
| 10. _____ house | J. aunt |
| 11. _____ land mass | K. mansion |
| 12. _____ laugh | L. cumulus |
| 13. _____ literature | M. sitar |
| 14. _____ medicine | N. incisor |
| 15. _____ musical instrument | O. biology |
| 16. _____ planet | P. guffaw |
| 17. _____ relative | Q. Uranus |
| 18. _____ science | R. aspirin |
| 19. _____ song | S. tiger |
| 20. _____ tooth | T. jogging |

Synonym for happy: ______________________

Sound: ______________________

Hairstyle: ______________________

Man's first name: ______________________

Name ______________________ Date __________ Period __________

# 1-40. FROM GENERAL TO SPECIFIC

The words in these ten groups of words can be placed in order from the most general to the most specific word/term within the group. The words in the first group have already been placed in that order for you. For the other nine groups, write the words from the most general to the most specific on the line below the group. On the lines below number 10, make up 3 examples like the ones you see here.

1. automobile sedan Toyota Toyota Camry
2. clams edibles seafood steamers

______________________________________________

3. sea vessel ship transportation vehicle *USS Constitution*

______________________________________________

4. elation emotion euphoria happiness

______________________________________________

5. female crossing guard lady person woman worker

______________________________________________

6. historical fiction literature novel *The Killer Angels*

______________________________________________

7. ballad "Big Bad John" music rock-and-roll

______________________________________________

8. liquid non-cola refreshment Seven-Up® soft drink

______________________________________________

9. magazine reading material *Time* weekly magazine

______________________________________________

10. head wear man's hat religious garb yarmulke

______________________________________________

______________________________________________

______________________________________________

Name ______________________ Date __________ Period __________

# 1-41. FROM GENERAL TO MORE SPECIFIC TO MOST SPECIFIC

Divide these 45 names into groups of three. Within each group, write the word that is general, the word that is more specific, and the word that is most specific. Thus, using the names listed below, a general word is *leader*, a more specific word is *president*, and the most specific word in that threesome is *Abraham Lincoln*.

Write the remaining 42 words in their appropriate columns. Each word/term is used only once.

Abraham Lincoln—animal—bed—body of water—body part—book—Cadillac—camera—car—comedy program—daisy—dog—dramatist—exercise—finger—flower—food—furniture— highway—index finger—Irish setter—leader—machine—meat—ocean—Pacific—plant—president—reading material—relative—road—Route 95—running—*Seinfeld*—Shakespeare— sprinting—steak—television program—*To Kill a Mockingbird*—twin—uncle—Uncle Rick—vehicle—video camera—writer

| *General* | *More Specific* | *Most Specific* |
|---|---|---|
| leader | president | Abraham Lincoln |
| ____________ | ____________ | ____________ |
| ____________ | ____________ | ____________ |
| ____________ | ____________ | ____________ |
| ____________ | ____________ | ____________ |
| ____________ | ____________ | ____________ |
| ____________ | ____________ | ____________ |
| ____________ | ____________ | ____________ |
| ____________ | ____________ | ____________ |
| ____________ | ____________ | ____________ |
| ____________ | ____________ | ____________ |
| ____________ | ____________ | ____________ |
| ____________ | ____________ | ____________ |
| ____________ | ____________ | ____________ |
| ____________ | ____________ | ____________ |

Name ______________________ Date __________ Period __________

# 1-42. IS IT GENERAL, MORE SPECIFIC, OR MOST SPECIFIC?

Consider the three terms *entertainment, movie,* and *The Lost World. Entertainment* is a general term. *Movie* is more specific. *The Lost World* is most specific. A writer who uses specifics allows the reader to become more involved in the reading process. That is an important goal in creating stories and essays.

In the line next to each term, write *general, more specific,* or *most specific.* Since the answers may vary, compare your answers with those of your classmates. Good discussion will ensue!

1. ______________ school subject
2. ______________ store
3. ______________ *Rocky*
4. ______________ winter
5. ______________ sport
6. ______________ Art 101
7. ______________ Pace University
8. ______________ Missouri River
9. ______________ song
10. ______________ yo-yo
11. ______________ candy
12. ______________ breakfast cereal
13. ______________ Dr. Seuss
14. ______________ Nevada
15. ______________ teacher
16. ______________ mammal
17. ______________ vegetable
18. ______________ Yellowstone Park
19. ______________ Hostess Twinkies™
20. ______________ pet

Name ______________________ Date __________ Period __________

# 1-43. CAN YOU BE MORE SPECIFIC, PLEASE?

Specific words are important for both the writer and the reader. Selecting the most precise word can help the writer be more exact and can help the reader better understand the writer's intentions.

Each of the 10 more general words below is followed by 4 more specific words that have been scrambled. Unscramble these 40 words and write their correct spellings on the line below. To help you along, each of the more precise word's first letter is underlined and its last letter is bold.

| | | | | |
|---|---|---|---|---|
| 1. DIG | powl | ubrorw | hnecanl | heo |
| | ________ | ________ | ________ | ________ |
| 2. HAPPY | lgdthdiee | eldeta | trlhiedl | uerocihp |
| | ________ | ________ | ________ | ________ |
| 3. HOUSE | cbain | tcsela | octtgae | nrcah |
| | ________ | ________ | ________ | ________ |
| 4. TRY | vneuter | eedanvor | sesay | tatetpm |
| | ________ | ________ | ________ | ________ |
| 5. WIN | rtuhipm | oqcunre | usdbeu | vnauqshi |
| | ________ | ________ | ________ | ________ |
| 6. THINK | noerdp | rseano | ereltfc | mdtateie |
| | ________ | ________ | ________ | ________ |
| 7. SMELLY | rkeye | oful | rcidan | dpirut |
| | ________ | ________ | ________ | ________ |
| 8. LOOK | eexniam | riewev | ansc | peintcs |
| | ________ | ________ | ________ | ________ |
| 9. SAD | glyomo | dessepder | dejdetec | casdowtn |
| | ________ | ________ | ________ | ________ |
| 10. FAMOUS | rewnedno | celratedeb | prentomin | ednot |
| | ________ | ________ | ________ | ________ |

Name ______________________ Date __________ Period __________

# 1-44. UNSCRAMBLING THE SPECIFICS

The group's heading appears above the four members of each group. Unscramble the letters of the four specific words in each group and write the answers in the spaces adjacent to them.

### *Animals*

akgonoar ____________________

ifgfear ____________________

epeltnah ____________________

greit ____________________

### *Body Parts*

lewbo ____________________

ahrte ____________________

nkela ____________________

ncke ____________________

### *Occupations*

etrehca ____________________

msona ____________________

aihctcetr ____________________

itrerw ____________________

### *Land Formations*

edrste ____________________

lavlye ____________________

omtnniau ____________________

vrniea ____________________

### *Reading Material*

nvole ____________________

mgeaniza ____________________

joalrnu ____________________

npeawserp ____________________

### *School Subjects*

gElnhsi ____________________

mtha ____________________

cencesi ____________________

ihstoyr ____________________

### *Sports*

voalllbley ____________________

osercc ____________________

netnis ____________________

obtllafo ____________________

### *Vehicles*

ldse ____________________

auleoibtom ____________________

arint ____________________

rukct ____________________

Name ______________________________ Date __________ Period __________

# 1-45. FISHING AROUND FOR SOME CORRECT ANSWERS

These six groups of words test your vocabulary skills. Each group's category is followed by four specific examples. Unscramble each category's four words and write each answer on the line next to the scrambled form of the word. The circled letters will be used to spell the special word for each category. Unscramble the letters and write this four-letter word on the line at the end of each list. After you have formed each group's word, you will know why this activity has this particular title.

***Fashion Statements***

_____stylish_____ t(s)shily

__________________ elean(t)g

__________________ r(n)deefi

__________________ av(e)su

__________________

***Friends***

__________________ muc(h)

__________________ c(o)ntidanf

__________________ (o)yncr

__________________ s(k)kicide

__________________

***How We Walk***

__________________ st(i)edr

__________________ (t)slolr

__________________ nuter(a)s

__________________ ael(b)m

__________________

***Moods***

__________________ ione(l)at

__________________ ho(i)areup

__________________ hais(n)epsp

__________________ rr(e)aupt

__________________

***Quarrels***

__________________ diutes(p)

__________________ tbreak(o)u

__________________ abbsq(e)lu

__________________ ge(l)wran

__________________

***Airborne Objects***

__________________ (c)doul

__________________ irigible(d)

__________________ (k)tei

__________________ rktec(o)

__________________

Name ______________________ Date __________ Period __________

# 1-46. LET'S GET A MORE EXACT WORD

Giving the reader the best possible picture of what is happening in your story is an important goal. Rather than merely saying "He *walked* across the room," you could use verbs such as *strutted*, *strolled*, *sauntered*, *hurried*, or *ambled* to give a better picture of how the character walked across the room.

The 15 verbs below are too general. On the line after each verb, write at least two verbs that more clearly express how the character performs the action. Compare and discuss your answers with your classmates.

1. throw ______________________
2. smile ______________________
3. talk ______________________
4. see ______________________
5. smell ______________________
6. taste ______________________
7. cook ______________________
8. touch ______________________
9. work ______________________
10. entertain ______________________
11. read ______________________
12. laugh ______________________
13. think ______________________
14. jump ______________________
15. cut ______________________

Name ______________________ Date __________ Period __________

# 1-47. LET'S TALK IT UP

We often use the word **said** in our writings; yet, we do not want to be repetitive. How many times can we write the word **said** before our readers start to yawn? Maintaining a reader's interest is an important goal.

Here are 15 words that resemble the word **said.** On the line following each word, write its meaning showing how it is different from the other 14 words. On the back of this sheet, write an illustrative paragraph using at least 10 of these words to show you know the words' meanings. Use your dictionary when necessary.

1. converse ______________________
2. consult: ______________________
3. discuss: ______________________
4. consider: ______________________
5. gossip: ______________________
6. relate: ______________________
7. babble: ______________________
8. chitchat: ______________________
9. address: ______________________
10. declare: ______________________
11. advise: ______________________
12. inform: ______________________
13. vent: ______________________
14. enlighten: ______________________
15. digress: ______________________

Name ______________________________ Date __________ Period __________

# 1-48. USAGE SITUATIONS

For each sentence, underline the correct word and then—on the line—write the correct word's letter as indicated by the number in parentheses after the sentence. Thus, for the first sentence, since the answer is *amount* and the number in parentheses is 6, letter *t*,—the sixth letter of the correct choice—has been written on the line. If you are correct for all sentences, the letters will spell a quotation.

1. _____ We could not assess the (amount, number) of damage the storm caused. **(6)**
2. __t__ "Your (childish, childlike) behavior will not be tolerated," said the coach. **(6)**
3. _____ The children enjoyed (theirselves, themselves) skating at the local rink. **(4)**
4. _____ What (affect, effect) will this decision have on your plans? **(1)**
5. _____ Gina is taller (than, then) her older sister. **(3)**
6. _____ A successful business usually has intelligent (personal, personnel). **(7)**
7. _____ His mother has not looked (good, well) since her hospital stay four months ago. **(4)**
8. _____ That material tends to (aggravate, irritate) her skin. **(5)**
9. _____ Please take that remark as a (complement, compliment). **(6)**
10. _____ This computer has many (good, well) features. **(4)**
11. _____ Before he became the president of the group, Ken Morris had (formally, formerly) been the association's representative. **(5)**
12. _____ Her mural on the gymnasium's wall was received quite (good, well) by the community members. **(1)**
13. _____ What (criteria, criterion) influence the junior class voters? **(8)**
14. _____ The train conductor was (disinterested, uninterested) in hearing our complaints. **(3)**
15. _____ Professor Thompson is an (eminent, imminent) historian. **(7)**
16. _____ Paulette, the class salutatorian, certainly (differs from, differs with) the other students who take a cavalier attitude towards hard work. **(8)**
17. _____ Luckily, the victim was (conscience, conscious) after the accident. **(7)**
18. _____ Did you know the (amount, number) of awards she received for her performance in that television program? **(6)**
19. _____ We decided to divide the responsibilities (among, between) the four workers. **(4)**
20. _____ I forgot that Augusta is the (capital, capitol) of Maine. **(6)**
21. _____ The rope that was too (loose, lose) caused many problems. **(3)**
22. _____ We were elected to serve on the school's (council, consul). **(4)**
23. _____ A lawyer is also referred to as a (council, counsel). **(6)**

The quotation: ______________________________________________________________

______________________________________________________________________

Name ______________________________ Date __________ Period __________

# 1-49. NOTING THE DIFFERENCE

Skillful writers are aware of how words differ. They know that although *ambling, strutting,* and *mincing* are all ways of walking, these words differ from one another. As a result, authors will choose the best word for their purposes. Using the exact word adds to a writer's effectiveness.

Each group below includes words that are closely related to one another. How are the words in each group different from one another? In the space provided, define each word, noting how it differs from the other words. Use your dictionary when necessary.

**Group One: ROADS** (a) boulevard (b) expressway (c) rotary

(a) ______________________________

(b) ______________________________

(c) ______________________________

**Group Two: INSTRUCTORS** (a) teacher (b) professor (c) instructor

(a) ______________________________

(b) ______________________________

(c) ______________________________

**Group Three: PERSONALITY DESCRIBERS** (a) proud (b) contented (c) conceited

(a) ______________________________

(b) ______________________________

(c) ______________________________

**Group Four: ACTIONS** (a) tease (b) harass (c) torment (d) pester

(a) ______________________________

(b) ______________________________

(c) ______________________________

(d) ______________________________

**Group Five: HUMORISTS** (a) clown (b) jokester (c) lampooner

(a) ______________________________

(b) ______________________________

(c) ______________________________

Name ______________________________ Date __________ Period __________

# 1-50. WHEN DO WE JOG? WHEN DO WE SPRINT?

A writer strives to be exact by selecting the most precise word to fit the occasion. If an author wants to describe the strong rain, the word *torrent* is more precise than the word *shower*. The more exact word tells the reader much more.

For each pair of words below, circle the higher degree word. Then, on the back of this sheet, show you know the difference between the pair's two words by writing a sentence for each one.

1. chuckle guffaw
2. jog sprint
3. mar ruin
4. pierce poke
5. peruse read
6. idolize love
7. coerce persuade
8. hurl toss
9. riot squabble
10. ogle scan
11. brush fire conflagration
12. minuscule small
13. hilarious silly
14. cool frigid
15. torrid warm
16. fat obese
17. obnoxious unpleasant
18. display flaunt
19. dainty finicky
20. slap wallop

Name ______________________ Date __________ Period __________

# 1-51. CLOSE . . . BUT DIFFERENT

These 17 questions feature pairs of words that are often misunderstood or confused. Circle the correct answer in each question and then write the correct word's corresponding letter in the space after the question's number. If you have answered these questions correctly, you will spell out the names of three land formations. Write those three names in the spaces at the bottom of this page.

1. _____ Which pertains to the legal system? (S) judicial (T) mien
2. _____ Which is a break or opening? (T) breach (U) breech
3. _____ What do you do if you fail to notice? (D) oversee (E) overlook
4. _____ Who is the person concerned with helping mankind? (O) humanist (P) humanitarian
5. _____ Which measures air pressure? (P) barometer (Q) thermometer
6. _____ Which is more than needed? (E) excess (F) access
7. _____ Which is the side of the ship next to the dock? (T) port (U) starboard
8. _____ Which is the dictionary definition of a word? (T) connotation (U) denotation
9. _____ Are things divided (M) between (N) among the seven people?
10. _____ Is an ocean part of a sea? (C) yes (D) no
11. _____ What does an odometer measure? (R) mileage (S) speed
12. _____ Who lives in an apartment? (A) tenant (B) tenet
13. _____ Which is the more accepted form of the word? (P) ketchup (Q) catsup
14. _____ Which is the longer version of a book? (K) abridged (L) unabridged
15. _____ If an object is fixed in one place, is it (A) stationary (B) stationery?
16. _____ Which is the higher honor at graduation? (H) magna cum laude (I) summa cum laude
17. _____ Which is the outline of a single course in school? (M) curriculum (N) syllabus

Three land formations: ______________________________________________

______________________________________________________________

Name ______________________________ Date __________ Period __________

# 1-52. THERE IS A DIFFERENCE

Here are words that are closely related and will test your word sense. Circle the word that correctly completes the sentence. Then, for each correct answer, write that word's letters that correspond to the numbers found in the parentheses after each sentence. Thus, since the first answer is *number* and the numbers in the parentheses are *1* and *2*, the *first* and *second* letters of the word *number* are written on the line.

Check your answers by writing the letters of the correct answers in consecutive order in the appropriate spaces at the bottom of this sheet. **Note:** In some instances the choices are not real words.

1. nu The (amount, number) of wedding pictures we ordered was nearly 50. **(1,2)**
2. ___ Unfortunately, the loud music (annoyed, aggravated) some of the people at the wedding. **(1,2)**
3. ___ Each table had olives, radishes, and (celery, salary) on the plates. **(1,2)**
4. ___ One of the guests at our table made an (allusion, illusion) to a Grisham novel. **(1,2)**
5. ___ The setting of the wedding reception was prettier (than, then) I had imagined. **(3,4)**
6. ___ Each table's floral arrangement was a (sensory, sensual) pleasure. **(4,5)**
7. ___ The bride wore a dress made by the (famous, infamous) designer who was hailed around the world as a fine person. **(1,2)**
8. ___ (Regardless, Irregardless) of the rain, the guests had a wonderful time. **(1,2)**
9. ___ The tips were divided (among, between) the 30 waiters and waitresses. **(1,2)**
10. ___ The new bride and groom posed for pictures with others and also by (theirselves, themselves). **(3,4)**
11. ___ We were amazed by the (amount, number) of concern the hired help showed each guest. **(3,6)**
12. ___ None of the guests showed the least bit of (frustratedness, frustration) with the inclement weather. **(9,10,11)**

a shade (#1–3) ____________________; a man's first name (#4–5) ____________________; a piece of furniture (#6–7) ____________________; a quantity of paper (#8–9) ____________________; a feeling(#10–12) ____________________

Name ______________________ Date __________ Period __________

# 1-53. POSITIVE AND NEGATIVE CONNOTATIONS

A connotation is an idea or notion suggested by a word. The word *belief* has a positive connotation while the word *delusion*, which is also a belief, has a negative connotation. Match the 20 words in the *Positive Connotations* column with the 20 words in the *Negative Connotations* column by writing the two-letter combination from the negatives column on the line next to the matching positives. The first answer is done for you. If your answers are correct, you will spell out two synonyms for the word *positive* and two synonyms for the word *negative*.

| *Positive Connotations* | *Negative Connotations* |
|---|---|
| 1. _af_ belief | delusion **(af)** |
| 2. _____ care | conceited **(at)** |
| 3. _____ chat | glut **(co)** |
| 4. _____ confident | interrogate **(ct)** |
| 5. _____ correct | nosy **(di)** |
| 6. _____ critical | carping **(ec)** |
| 7. _____ different | grotesque **(er)** |
| 8. _____ disregard | anxiety **(fi)** |
| 9. _____ effort | pains **(in)** |
| 10. _____ fill | avenge **(iv)** |
| 11. _____ fragrance | covet **(li)** |
| 12. _____ husky | immature **(ng)** |
| 13. _____ interested | skinny **(nn)** |
| 14. _____ question | odor **(nt)** |
| 15. _____ save | hoard **(or)** |
| 16. _____ see | obese **(ra)** |
| 17. _____ slender | gossip **(rm)** |
| 18. _____ sound | flout **(ta)** |
| 19. _____ wish | blare **(ul)** |
| 20. _____ youthful | espy **(ya)** |

Two synonyms for positive: ______________________________.

Two synonyms for negative: ______________________________.

Name ______________________________ Date __________ Period __________

# 1-54. THE GOOD AND THE BAD

The following 20 words share something in common: they are all negative words. But don't despair! Their positive counterparts are found under the **Favorable** column below. Write the unfavorable (negative) word in the space next to its favorable partner. The first one is done for you.

| | | | |
|---|---|---|---|
| arrogant | dearth | grimace | narrow-minded |
| bland | deluge | guffaw | ornate |
| blare | eyesore | hovel | spastic |
| chaotic | failure | indigent | strangle |
| coarse | fallow | ludicrous | trudge |

| *Category* | *Favorable* | *Unfavorable* |
|---|---|---|
| 1. sound | toot | blare |
| 2. movement description | agile | ______________ |
| 3. touch | caress | ______________ |
| 4. taste | savory | ______________ |
| 5. laugh | chuckle | ______________ |
| 6. sight | vision | ______________ |
| 7. idea | sensible | ______________ |
| 8. house | mansion | ______________ |
| 9. style | adorned | ______________ |
| 10. financial status | affluent | ______________ |
| 11. outcome | success | ______________ |
| 12. precipitation | shower | ______________ |
| 13. mouth's movement | smile | ______________ |
| 14. situation | orderly | ______________ |
| 15. personal trait | charitable | ______________ |
| 16. supply | plethora | ______________ |
| 17. type of walk | glide | ______________ |
| 18. texture | smooth | ______________ |
| 19. land | productive | ______________ |
| 20. attitude | open-minded | ______________ |

Name ______________________________ Date ___________ Period ___________

# 1-55. COMPLETING THE QUOTE

The words of some famous men and women are cited below. One word from each person's quote is missing. Using the contextual clues of the sentence, fill in the blank with one of the words in the box. Each word is used once. Discuss your answers with your classmates.

| | | |
|---|---|---|
| abuse | fate | lies |
| defect | generous | refreshment |
| consent | geography | time |
| elders | imitation | vices |

1. "No one can make you feel inferior without your ______________________." (*Eleanor Roosevelt*)
2. "Young men have a passion for regarding their ______________________ as senile." (*Henry Adams*)
3. "Whipping and ______________________ are like laudanum; you have to double the dose as the sensibilities decline." (*Harriet Beecher Stowe*)
4. "Without ______________________ humanity would perish of despair and boredom." (*Anatole France*)
5. "In the mind and nature of a man a secret is an ugly thing, like a hidden physical ______________________." (*Isak Dinesen*)
6. "History is all explained by ______________________." (*Robert Penn Warren*)
7. "______________________ in its aging course teaches all things." (*Aeschylus*)
8. "Search others for their virtues, thy self for thy ______________________." (*Ben Franklin*)
9. "If a man is prodigal, he cannot be truly ______________________." (*James Boswell*)
10. "To sit in the shade on a fine day and look upon verdure is the most perfect ______________________." (*Jane Austen*)
11. "______________________ is the sincerest flattery." (*Charles Caleb Colton*)
12. "Whatever limits us we call ______________________." (*Ralph Waldo Emerson*)

SECTION FOUR

# USING WORDS EFFECTIVELY

Name ______________________________ Date __________ Period __________

# 1-56. DESCRIBING A CHARACTER

Much like the people we know in our daily lives, the characters we meet in literary works, theatrical productions, movies, and television shows possess certain traits. Some of these characteristics are worthy of our respect while others are less than admirable. What qualities of your favorite comic book hero or your movie heroine do you admire? Which literary character makes you uncomfortable or repulsed? Why?

Using the acrostic form shown below in the Huck Finn example, write the names of five fictional characters you have encountered. For each letter of that character's name (include both the first and last names if you want), write a quality of that character starting with that specific letter. Be prepared to cite an instance that exemplifies that trait. Use the other side of this sheet if necessary.



**Example character: Huck Finn**

H . . . honest U . . . uncultured C . . . concerned K . . . kind

F . . . friendly I . . . informal N . . . naïve N . . . nonviolent

**Character #1:** ______________________________

______________________________

______________________________

______________________________

**Character #2:** ______________________________

______________________________

______________________________

______________________________

**Character #3:** ______________________________

______________________________

______________________________

______________________________

**Character #4:** ______________________________

______________________________

______________________________

______________________________

**Character #5:** ______________________________

______________________________

______________________________

______________________________

Name ______________________________ Date __________ Period __________

# 1-57. MATCHING THE MASTERS

Imitating good writers is helpful in your becoming an effective writer. Observing their style, including their word choice, is instructive and potentially beneficial to you. This activity features excerpts from five famous writers. In each case, several words from the text have been deleted and replaced with blank lines. Based on the context of the excerpt, fill in each blank with a word that you feel is appropriate. Compare your answers with those of your classmates. Be ready to support your word choices. Your teacher has the deleted words so that you can see how you matched up with the masters!

(1) "She was a __________________ young woman, with dark, __________________ hair cropped and __________________ on the side, a short, __________________ face with straight __________________, and a large curved mouth."—Katherine Anne Porter from "Old Mortality"

(2) "He is a __________________ gypsy in aspect, in __________________ and __________________ a gentleman: that is, as much a gentleman as a country __________________; rather __________________, perhaps, yet not __________________with his negligence, because he has an __________________ and __________________ figure..."—Emily Bronte from "Wuthering Heights"

(3) "She had on __________________ shorts with __________________ stripes and red __________________ with white __________________ and a sleeveless T-shirt with a picture of Margaret Mead the anthropologist on it. Her red __________________ in the ponytail __________________ all over the place like a fire __________________ her down the __________________."—Michael Malone from "Fast Love"

(4) "His face was the face of a __________________—thin and ascetic, but his __________________ had the __________________ gleam of the fanatic. They were __________________ and thoughtful, the eyes of a man who is __________________ to looking at death."—Liam O'Flaherty from "The Sniper"

(5) "He inherited, __________________, but little of the martial character of his ancestors. He was a__________________, good-natured man; he was, __________________, a kind neighbor and an __________________ henpecked __________________."
—Washington Irving from "Rip Van Winkle"

Name ______________________ Date __________ Period __________

# 1-58. ADJECTIVES RELATED TO OUR SENSES

Your five senses are important. Describing what you have seen, touched, heard, smelled, or tasted is a skill you will need as a writer. Using sensory adjectives such as *spicy*, *hot*, and *saucy* to describe a slice of pizza allows your reader to have a more complete idea of the pizza.

Each sense is given its own column below. One word for each sense has been given to you. Fill in the blank spaces with words appropriate to that sense. Then write 5 sentences—1 for each of the *smell* words you have used on the lines below.

| ***Sight*** | ***Touch*** | ***Sound*** | ***Smell*** | ***Taste*** |
|---|---|---|---|---|
| beautiful | brittle | loud | fragrant | sour |
| ______ | ______ | ______ | ______ | ______ |
| ______ | ______ | ______ | ______ | ______ |
| ______ | ______ | ______ | ______ | ______ |
| ______ | ______ | ______ | ______ | ______ |
| ______ | ______ | ______ | ______ | ______ |

______________________________________________

______________________________________________

______________________________________________

______________________________________________

______________________________________________

Name ______________________ Date __________ Period __________

# 1-59. ILLUSTRATING A PERSON'S CHARACTERISTICS

By using specific examples, effective writers convey much about their characters. In the sentence "The manager refused to accept the umpire's decision," the reader knows that the manager is certainly unhappy, or perhaps stubborn. What other characteristics can be attributed to the manager based on this sentence?

For each of the following 15 characteristics, write an illustrative sentence that clearly exemplifies that trait. Use the sentence above as your guide.

1. affluent ______________________
2. belligerent ______________________
3. caring ______________________
4. curious ______________________
5. depressed ______________________
6. egocentric ______________________
7. frustrated ______________________
8. gentle ______________________
9. hardworking ______________________
10. honest ______________________
11. humorous ______________________
12. intelligent ______________________
13. interesting ______________________
14. introverted ______________________
15. nervous ______________________

Name ______________________ Date __________ Period __________

# 1-60. MOOD INDICATORS

Writers relate much about a character by describing the character's actions. How a character walks, talks, scratches his head, or moves her arm can help the reader know the character better. Read each sentence below. Then on the line beneath each sentence, write what the author intended us to know about the character through the underlined portion of each sentence. Compare your answers with those of your classmates. Be prepared to support your choices.

1. <u>With a dubious look on his face</u>, the spokesperson approached the microphone.

   ______________________________

2. The young lady <u>was nodding her head</u> as the foreman gave her directions.

   ______________________________

3. <u>His guffaw</u> could be heard across the crowded room.

   ______________________________

4. Jerry heard his father's ultimatum and <u>rolled his eyes</u> as he walked back to his bedroom.

   ______________________________

5. The group received the news of the company's plans <u>with skepticism</u>.

   ______________________________

6. <u>With his teeth chattering</u>, the man who had been trapped in the snow for thirty hours greeted his family.

   ______________________________

7. <u>Craning her neck</u>, Tammy tried to hear the speaker's words.

   ______________________________

8. The older man <u>was cupping his hands behind his ears</u> as his grandson's address was delivered.

   ______________________________

9. My mother had <u>a look of incredulity on her face</u> as she heard the news.

   ______________________________

10. We saw the cowboy <u>gritting his teeth</u> as he tried to rope the steer.

    ______________________________

11. He <u>raised his eyebrows</u> at us as we all listened to Harold's story.

    ______________________________

12. <u>Biting his fingernails</u>, Leo was in the dentist's waiting room.

    ______________________________

13. Rudolfo <u>was glaring</u> at his opponent.

    ______________________________

14. Before diving from the highest board, the stunt woman <u>took a deep breath</u>.

    ______________________________

15. He <u>stealthily</u> entered the darkened room while his friend guarded the door.

    ______________________________

Name ______________________ Date __________ Period __________

# 1-61. THE RESPONSE

Why would you probably be unhappy if someone responded to you in a *brusque* manner? Would it be better if you received a *flippant* answer? How would a *disparaging* response compare with these other two?

This activity asks you to differentiate how people respond to other people. Using your dictionary, write an illustrative sentence that shows your understanding of each of the 15 words below. Discuss your answers with your classmates.

1. ambivalent ______________________
2. brusque ______________________
3. candid ______________________
4. caustic ______________________
5. conciliatory ______________________
6. condescending ______________________
7. contrite ______________________
8. critical ______________________
9. disparaging ______________________
10. ebullient ______________________
11. flippant ______________________
12. gracious ______________________
13. petulant ______________________
14. sincere ______________________
15. superficial ______________________

Name ______________________ Date __________ Period __________

# 1-62. USING MORE SPECIFIC VERBS

Using the words from the box below, replace each underlined portion of the sentence with one of those 15 words. Write the correct word on the line before each sentence. Each word is used only once.

1. ______________________ The building fell down yesterday.
2. ______________________ Frankie hurt his knee yesterday when he was skateboarding.
3. ______________________ The minister talked from the pulpit for fifteen minutes.
4. ______________________ Several tired soldiers walked back to the camp.
5. ______________________ We saw that the tall, skinny miler had run the last fifty yards of the race.
6. ______________________ My uncle cleaned the stain out of my shirt.
7. ______________________ The swimmer moved her arms quickly as she tried to ward off the attacker.
8. ______________________ All the chorus members sang together beautifully before the concert.
9. ______________________ Four of the criminal investigators looked into the possible motives for the crime.
10. ______________________ During the play some of the audience members laughed slyly at the actor's movements.
11. ______________________ Leslie solved the cryptic message by herself.
12. ______________________ My social studies teacher told of the days of the Great Depression.
13. ______________________ The camper really did not like getting up so early in the morning.
14. ______________________ One of the boys on line gently pushed his friend in front of him.
15. ______________________ Having just figured out the answer, the mathematician rechecked her computations.

| | | |
|---|---|---|
| calculated | nudged | scrubbed |
| collapsed | preached | snickered |
| decoded | probed | sprinted |
| harmonized | recalled | thrashed |
| loathed | scraped | trudged |

Name ______________________ Date __________ Period __________

# 1-63. DESCRIBING YOUR SURROUNDINGS

Using the most exact words or phrases, describe each of these people, places, things, or ideas. Be as specific as possible. The answers do not have to be in complete sentences. Use the other side of this sheet if necessary. Share your answers with your classmates.

1. the shoes you are wearing today ______________________
2. the area immediately outside your English classroom ______________________
3. the outfit you have on now ______________________
4. your favorite CD cover ______________________
5. a rainy Monday morning ______________________
6. the school hallway at dismissal ______________________
7. qualities you look for in a movie ______________________
8. a favorite relative ______________________
9. your best sweater ______________________
10. a park near you ______________________
11. a friend's face ______________________
12. an important street in your neighborhood ______________________

Name ______________________ Date __________ Period __________

# 1-64. EXPRESSING YOURSELF THROUGH CLOTHING

We will *take our hats off to you* and you will get *a feather in your cap* if you can explain each of the 20 underlined expressions below. All of these common expressions include an article of clothing. On the back of this sheet, write each expression's meaning. If there is time, look up the origins of these expressions. Compare your answers with those of your classmates.

1. He played his cards close to the vest.
2. Ned had a few tricks up his sleeve.
3. The politician had that group of voters in her hip pocket.
4. I must take my hat off to you for that.
5. Kenny was shaking in his boots at the sight of that.
6. That was a real feather in Olivia's cap!
7. He tells everyone that he wears the pants in that family, but we know the truth.
8. Carolyn's uncle is a man of the cloth.
9. Our class leader, Matt Newman, wears many hats.
10. The president used the pocket veto in that instance.
11. Friday is dress down day at my mother's office.
12. We should play dress up and act silly for awhile.
13. We have never been invited to a black-tie affair.
14. After hearing the news of his grandfather's death, Nick purchased a mourning suit.
15. He was never one to talk through his hat.
16. You should walk in another's shoes before you say something like that.
17. I would keep it under my hat if I were you.
18. Now the shoe is on the other foot.
19. This is where the shoe pinches.
20. He found it hard to fill the shoes of his father.

Name ______________________ Date __________ Period __________

# 1-65. DON'T GET HYPER, BIG CHEESE!

Words have their distinctions. Knowing the difference between slang and informal language is important to you as a writer. Slang is "the highly informal speech outside the conventional or standard way of speaking." Slang's usage consists of coined terms and extended meanings of established terms. Informal language is defined as "colloquial words and phrases in widespread use and characteristic of conversation and informal writing." Thus, for the word *daze*, its informal equivalent is *bowl over* and its slang equivalent is *blow one away*.

Using the following words and phrases, write the correct informal and slang equivalents in the proper columns.

**Informal:** bowl over; chip in; fly off; get out from under; holler; hyper; info; kingpin; pile it on,; prep; shake off; suck in; throw a curve; turn one's stomach; wallop

**Slang:** antsy; beat the rap; belt out; big cheese; blow one away; conk; dish out; dope; foul up; gross out; knock off; psyche oneself up; shoot off one's mouth; shoot the bull; snooker

| *Word* | *Informal* | *Slang* |
|---|---|---|
| daze | bowl over | blow one away |
| entangle | ____________ | ____________ |
| evade | ____________ | ____________ |
| exaggerate | ____________ | ____________ |
| finish | ____________ | ____________ |
| horrify | ____________ | ____________ |
| leader | ____________ | ____________ |
| mislead | ____________ | ____________ |
| nervous | ____________ | ____________ |
| news | ____________ | ____________ |
| pay | ____________ | ____________ |
| prepare | ____________ | ____________ |
| punch | ____________ | ____________ |
| rant | ____________ | ____________ |
| shout | ____________ | ____________ |

Name ______________________ Date __________ Period __________

# 1-66. EXPRESSING YOURSELF WITH EXPRESSIONS

*When the group members had to make their eleventh-hour decision, they knew the handwriting was on the wall. Out on a limb, each member, none wet behind the ears, had to knuckle down and refuse to throw in the towel.*

The above short paragraph contains 6 expressions that appear below. Match the 20 expressions in Column A with their meanings in Column B by writing the corresponding letter on the line next to the correct expression.

| ***Column A (Expressions)*** | ***Column B (Meanings)*** |
|---|---|
| 1. _____ below the belt | A. apply oneself energetically and seriously |
| 2. _____ diddly-squat | B. avoiding extremes |
| 3. _____ eleventh hour | C. be suspicious |
| 4. _____ flash in the pan | D. control |
| 5. _____ get one's goat | E. divulge secret information |
| 6. _____ green-eyed monster | F. follow behind |
| 7. _____ handwriting on the wall | G. impending doom |
| 8. _____ knuckle down | H. in a risky position |
| 9. _____ lock, stock, and barrel | I. inexperienced |
| 10. _____ middle of the road | J. jealousy |
| 11. _____ out on a limb | K. the last time to make a decision |
| 12. _____ play second fiddle | L. to make angry or frustrated |
| 13. _____ rule the roost | M. meeting the usual standard |
| 14. _____ shot in the arm | N. person or thing successful for only a short time |
| 15. _____ smell a rat | O. quit |
| 16. _____ spill the beans | P. rich |
| 17. _____ throw in the towel | Q. sudden infusion of energy |
| 18. _____ up to snuff | R. unfair |
| 19. _____ well-heeled | S. very little of anything |
| 20. _____ wet behind the ears | T. wholeness |

Name ______________________ Date __________ Period __________

# 1-67. EXPRESSIONS USING BODY PARTS

Twenty common expressions are found within the sentences below. Fill in each blank with a body part that completes the sentence. A body part can be used more than once. Discuss what each expression means.

1. If I am unwilling to listen, I turn a deaf ____________________.
2. Bo said he would ____________________ the bill for our meal.
3. Leon did not want to pay an ____________________ and a ____________________ for the new car.
4. It was not wise for George to ____________________ off to the new principal.
5. I learned long ago to hold my ____________________ rather than say something I would later regret.
6. We thought we would pull Lisa's ____________________ with that practical joke.
7. Unfortunately, the class got off on the wrong ____________________ with the substitute teacher.
8. Please be careful and keep an ____________________ to the ground.
9. The tough game demanded that each player fight with ____________________ and ____________________.
10. It was important that the team captain keep his ____________________ and not lose his cool.
11. The elderly man was long in the ____________________.
12. The company's salesperson hoped to ____________________ down the deal by ten o'clock.
13. With her new hairstyle Marisa hoped to catch the handsome boy's ____________________.
14. No person really wants to be led by the ____________________ and have another control him or her.
15. You put yourself in that position because you bit your ____________________ to spite your ____________________.
16. Though the word was on the tip of her ____________________, she could not think of it in time.
17. His skills proved that he was ____________________ and ____________________ above the other competitors.
18. With such a strict boss, each worker had to ____________________ the line.
19. After such a long speech, we had to stretch our ____________________.
20. I am glad that you and I see ____________________ to ____________________ on this tough issue.

Name ______________________ Date __________ Period __________

# 1-68. FIT AS A FIDDLE WITH THESE EXPRESSIONS!

This activity is no chicken feed! Sit in the catbird seat and bring home the bacon by correctly explaining what each of the 20 underlined expressions means. Write your answers on the back of this sheet and then discuss your answers with your classmates.

1. Winning first place in the art contest was <u>a feather in the cap</u> for Michelle.
2. Could you please give us <u>a ballpark estimate</u> of the number of people in attendance last night?
3. He has a tendency <u>to gum up the</u> works when the pressure is on his group.
4. After his election victory James was <u>in the catbird seat</u>.
5. He would always tell us that as the family's financial supporter he was the one who <u>brought home the bacon</u>.
6. Francine noted that her coach would sometimes <u>fly off the handle</u>.
7. As far as the police officer was concerned, the matter was <u>cut and dried</u>.
8. Isn't it about time that you and they <u>bury the hatchet</u>?
9. This is where I <u>draw the line</u>!
10. Since this was not accepted by the committee, we are <u>back to square one</u>.
11. I have a feeling you will be <u>called on the carpet</u> for this blunder, Larry.
12. Both students admitted that they had been <u>caught red handed</u>.
13. Do you expect me to accept such <u>chicken feed</u> for an hourly wage?
14. He <u>went haywire</u> when I told him that Jeanine wanted to break up with him.
15. After we did not score a run in the next to last inning, the <u>handwriting was on the wall</u>.
16. Chemistry proved to be his <u>Achilles heel</u> this year.
17. They came to an <u>eleventh-hour</u> decision concerning the new music teacher.
18. To say the least, many of Mr. Lawrence's ideas on how life should be lived are <u>off the wall</u>.
19. Do not try <u>to pull a fast one</u> by handing in a term paper that someone else wrote last year.
20. Unfortunately, someone had to be the <u>scapegoat</u> for the others last night.

Name ______________________ Date __________ Period __________

# 1-69. NO MONKEYING AROUND HERE!

Do you enjoy the dog days of August? Do you know someone who has rabbit ears? When was the last time you were involved in a bull session? This activity allows for no monkeying around!

Each expression below includes an animal's name. Write the correct term on the line next to its appropriate definition.

| | | | |
|---|---|---|---|
| bird dog | chicken pox | goose step | pig Latin |
| bull session | crocodile tears | horseshoes | pigtail |
| bunny hop | dog days | kangaroo court | Pony Express |
| cat-o'-nine-tails | duckpins | monkey bars | rabbit ears |
| catwalk | fox trot | paper tiger | snake pit |

1. ______________________ children's playground equipment
2. ______________________ indoor television antennae
3. ______________________ informal discussion
4. ______________________ hot, uncomfortable days in July and August
5. ______________________ silly type of dance
6. ______________________ whip used for flogging
7. ______________________ dance for couples with a variety of fast and slow steps
8. ______________________ person who searches for new talent
9. ______________________ person who poses a threat that is ineffective
10. ______________________ insincere show of grief
11. ______________________ playful, secret language
12. ______________________ disease, usually of small children
13. ______________________ system used to carry and deliver mail
14. ______________________ army march
15. ______________________ long braid of hair
16. ______________________ game including the word "ringer"
17. ______________________ unauthorized session that disregards legal procedure
18. ______________________ place of horror and confusion
19. ______________________ game like bowling
20. ______________________ narrow, elevated walk or platform

Name ______________________________ Date __________ Period __________

# 1-70. SELECTING THE CORRECT WORD

These 15 sentences feature challenging questions regarding idioms, expressions, and other usage concerns. Underline the correct choice in each sentence. The first letter of each correct choice will help to spell out a three-letter word. Write each letter in the appropriate space at the bottom of this sheet. Thus, #1–3 is one word, #4–6 is another, and so forth. If you have answered the questions correctly, you will have spelled out 5 three-letter words.

1. Ben is similar (to, with) his brother.
2. They agree (on, to) the terms of the contract.
3. Kim enjoys waiting (at, on) customers in her aunt's diner.
4. Seldom is Marshall angry (at, with) others.
5. Yet, he was disappointed (by, in) the decision.
6. Marsha doesn't consider herself superior (of, to) her colleagues.
7. Dale's grandfather was oblivious (of, to) the road's dangerous curve.
8. At times Jose works independently (from, of) the other group members.
9. His handwriting is identical (from, to) his dad's.
10. We certainly differ (about, from) that decision.
11. How much did the waiter charge that woman (for, fore) that meal?
12. Prior (for, to) that, he did not ask me a single question.
13. What did Tom infer (from, with) your words?
14. Sean lives (at, in) California.
15. Will he abide (by, with) the new ruling?

The 5 three-letter words: ______________________________________________

________________________________________________________________

Name ______________________________ Date __________ Period __________

# 1-71. POSITIONING WORDS

To describe a character's emotions or situation, a writer relies upon words and expressions that the reader should know. Have you ever been in seventh heaven? Perhaps you have sat in the catbird seat? These are two expressions that writers use in their stories.

Select the correct answer for each expression by writing its corresponding letter in the space provided. Then, on the other side of this sheet, write an illustrative sentence showing your knowledge of the expression.

1. _____ *between a rock and a hard place:* (a) pleasurable situation (b) unenviable situation (c) enviable situation
2. _____ *at the top of her game:* (a) doing the best she has ever done (b) lost in a tough predicament (c) losing badly
3. _____ *at the point of no return:* (a) too deeply involved to withdraw (b) can't find a way back home (c) a failed adventure
4. _____ *in the driver's seat:* (a) out of control (b) looking for an answer (c) in control
5. _____ *in the pits:* (a) worst possible position or place (b) lost (c) best situation
6. _____ *in the catbird seat:* (a) enviable position, as of power (b) dangerous position (c) unlucky position
7. _____ *in seventh heaven:* (a) mentally unbalanced (b) questionable behavior (c) perfect happiness
8. _____ *Utopian society:* (a) place of disharmony (b) place of perfection (c) anarchy
9. _____ *on top of the world:* (a) very happy (b) different from normal (c) depressed
10. _____ *pinnacle of her career:* (a) highest point (b) lowest point (c) midpoint
11. _____ *crossroads of his life:* (a) near the end (b) in the middle (c) time in which important decisions must be made
12. _____ *in the doldrums:* (a) in high spirits (b) in low spirits (c) confused
13. _____ *on cloud nine:* (a) confused (b) tired (c) very happy
14. _____ *here and now:* (a) presently (b) everywhere (c) nowhere
15. _____ *wishy-washy answer:* (a) firm (b) weak (c) rude

Name ______________________________ Date __________ Period __________

# 1-72. REMOVING WORDS THAT ARE SUPERFLUOUS

The title is superfluous. It has too many words! Instead, the title could just as easily be "Remove Superfluous Words." In each sentence make the underlined section more concise by removing the superfluous words. Insert the changes in the space above each sentence.

1. I will visit the museum <u>the day after today</u>.
2. <u>In a very short time from now</u>, the bus will arrive.
3. Jason looked at the schedule <u>that tells when the bus will arrive</u>.
4. The <u>students in the class taught by Mrs. Chamberlain</u> will go on the field trip.
5. <u>At the Children's Museum located in Boston</u>, the class will spend two hours viewing the exhibits.
6. The tour guide <u>who is experienced in giving tours</u> will meet the class in the foyer.
7. <u>Not one of the students in Mrs. Chamberlain's</u> class will forget this class outing.
8. <u>Some of the exhibits found in the</u> museum will be rearranged next month.
9. The workers <u>who work at the museum were helpful and helped many people</u>.
10. For lunch, the children ate <u>in the large room called the cafeteria</u>.
11. All of the students were allowed to <u>roam around</u>.
12. The guide talked about the <u>frozen</u> ice of the ancient times.
13. We <u>saw the entire exhibit with our own eyes</u>.
14. She spoke of the <u>generous philanthropists who support the museum</u>.
15. We asked her about the <u>wandering nomads</u>.

Name ________________________________ Date __________ Period __________

# 1-73. WHEN TOO MANY WORDS ARE TOO MUCH

Good writers strive to be concise. Exactness and conciseness help the reader enjoy and appreciate good writing. This activity will help you become more concise in your writing.

Each sentence needs to be more concise. Some are redundant. On a separate sheet of paper, rewrite the sentence retaining as many of the details as possible. The word order can be rearranged. Discuss your answers with your classmates.

1. The man was arrested for igniting a fire.
2. We needed to consult a book that has synonyms for many words.
3. The lady who sings songs for a living has a voice that has great beauty.
4. Do not go beyond the limits of this property.
5. The female graduates of Smith College gave donations of money to Smith.
6. Raymond yelled loudly the day before today.
7. The criminal was accused of illegal transference of another's finances.
8. The burner that burns oil was repaired by the man whose job is to fix the apparatus.
9. It was apparent to my eyes that the man who works for the police department as a guy who patrols our neighborhood was in a mood similar to but not quite so much as euphoria.
10. An overindulgence in imbibing beverages made of alcohol can be detrimental to the general well-being of an individual.
11. A female person between the ages of 13 and 19 was observed by the male person named Mr. Munson who was operating a yellow vehicle carrying school children to their place of study driving her motor vehicle in a manner that surpassed the allowable number of miles per hour ordered by the mandates of the law enforcement authorities.

Name ______________________ Date __________ Period __________

# 1-74. ARE YOU A LENGOOL? DO YOU LENGOOL?

There is no such word as *lengool.* It was made up especially for this activity. What do you think the word *lengool* would mean if it were a real word? Does it have a positive or negative suggestion? Is it a noun? Is it a verb? Is it some other part of speech?

Have some fun and make up your own definition for each of these invented words. Compare your definitions with those of your classmates. Be ready to discuss why you feel the definition is appropriate to that word. What do your answers tell you about word connotations, the idea or notion suggested by or associated with a word?

1. lengool ______________________
2. hemmoliac ______________________
3. frontent ______________________
4. moost ______________________
5. yokism ______________________
6. tolp ______________________
7. slisnot ______________________
8. zerruchno ______________________
9. reduraram ______________________
10. elbatsnok ______________________
11. chasp ______________________
12. porpitude ______________________
13. norriby ______________________
14. ridan ______________________
15. romaf ______________________

Name ______________________________ Date __________ Period __________

# 1-75. HELPING OUT

Here is your opportunity to help to construct sentences. Read the sentences below and then write the word of your choice in each blank. Each word you supply should fit the sense of the sentence. Be ready to support your choices.

Sherry ____________________ walked into the ____________________ in the mall. Most of the ____________________ who were ____________________ stopped and looked at her. They were ____________________ by her appearance.

____________________ of the newspapers in their ____________________ were over two years old. The family members loved to ____________________ things that most other ____________________ would have ____________________ out long ago.

____________________ for his biting humor, the comedian enjoyed ____________________ fun at those who most ____________________ it. ____________________, he would find ____________________ in something that a ____________________ had said at a press conference. Then, similar ____________________ a ____________________, he would ____________________ his victim.

Last night my friend's ____________________ blew out when she was ____________________home from the ____________________ meeting. She ____________________ on my door at one-thirty in the morning and ____________________ if we ____________________ help her ____________________ the ____________________.

When the worker ____________________ her assistant ____________________ near the ____________________, she ____________________ called for ____________________. ____________________ several of the other people on the job ____________________ to the scene and ____________________ to ____________________ the injured man to ____________________.

Name ______________________ Date __________ Period __________

# 1-76. PLAYING WITH WORDS

How smart are you when it comes to detecting a pun, the literary term for a play on words? Using puns as your guide, match the 20 people listed in Column A with the 20 adverbs listed in Column B. Write the adverb's letter in the appropriate space next to the person who "said" it in that fashion. Thus, since the *artist* said it *colorfully*, the letter *D* is written next to *number 1*. Some of these puns are more obvious than others. Examine all the possibilities since some answers are closely related. The items in both columns are used only once



| ***Column A*** | ***Column B*** |
|---|---|
| 1. __D__ the artist said . . . | A. beautifully |
| 2. _____ the beautician said . . . | B. bravely |
| 3. _____ the bettor said . . . | C. childishly |
| 4. _____ the builder said . . . | D. colorfully |
| 5. _____ the chef said . . . | E. constructively |
| 6. _____ the conductor said . . . | F. cuttingly |
| 7. _____ the dieter said . . . | G. directly |
| 8. _____ the doctor said . . . | H. hotly |
| 9. _____ the dramatist said . . . | I. intelligently |
| 10. _____ the firefighter said . . . | J. laboriously |
| 11. _____ the genius said . . . | K. musically |
| 12. _____ the guitarist said . . . | L. oddly |
| 13. _____ the heroine said . . . | M. patiently |
| 14. _____ the lumberjack said . . . | N. playfully |
| 15. _____ the model said . . . | O. powerfully |
| 16. _____ the pediatrician said . . . | P. sparingly |
| 17. _____ the philosopher said . . . | Q. strikingly |
| 18. _____ the pitcher said . . . | R. stylistically |
| 19. _____ the weight lifter said . . . | S. tastefully |
| 20. _____ the worker said . . . | T. thoughtfully |

Section Five

# A POTPOURRI OF PUZZLES

| | | |
|---|---|---|
| 1–77 | IF THE HAT FITS | Vocabulary cryptology |
| 1–78 | OPPOSITES ATTRACT | Antonyms word-find |
| 1–79 | SPANNING THE ALPHABET | Vocabulary crossword |
| 1–80 | TEAMS OF THREE | Grouping word-find |
| 1–81 | CONNECTING THE PREFIX AND THE ROOT | Word construction fill-in-the-blank |
| 1–82 | YOU : WINNER | Analogy magic square |
| 1–83 | START WITH A VOWEL | Vocabulary crossword |
| 1–84 | SOMETHING IN COMMON | Specifics crossword |
| 1–85 | END WHERE YOU BEGAN | Word-fun crossword |
| 1–86 | X MARKS THE SPOT | Vocabulary crossword |
| 1–87 | SMALL'S SYNONYMS | Synonyms cryptology |
| 1–88 | SYNONYMS FOR BIG | Synonyms word-find |
| 1–89 | SYNONYMS FOR TALK | Synonyms cryptology |
| 1–90 | THREE'S COMPANY | Synonyms crossword |

Name ______________________ Date __________ Period __________

# 1-77. IF THE HAT FITS

Twenty types of head wear are concealed in this cryptolist. Find the letters that were substituted in the original word and write those letters in the appropriate lines. To help you along, the letter substitution code is started at the bottom of this sheet.

1. TNPBWPJNWPX = _ _ _ _ _ _ _ _ _ _ _
2. JVWOEV = _ _ _ _ _ _
3. BNHSV = _ _ _ _ _
4. BNRLWB = _ _ _ _ _ _
5. BVOZWGGNO = _ _ _ _ _ _ _ _ _
6. JVPVB = _ _ _ _ _
7. FWPTSGUV = _ _ _ _ _ _ _ _
8. LWPXLWB = _ _ _ _ _ _ _
9. JNMGVP = _ _ _ _ _ _
10. KWR = _ _ _
11. XVPJF = _ _ _ _ _
12. AVXNPW = _ _ _ _ _ _
13. OEZLBKWR = _ _ _ _ _ _ _ _
14. JEPVBBW = _ _ _ _ _ _ _
15. LVGTVB = _ _ _ _ _ _
16. YUSGGKWR = _ _ _ _ _ _ _ _
17. YBPWMLWB = _ _ _ _ _ _ _ _
18. BSPJWO = _ _ _ _ _ _
19. AVD = _ _ _
20. XSOKVKWR = _ _ _ _ _ _ _ _

*Letter Substitution Code Used:*

| Letter: | A | B | C | D | E | F | G | H | I | J | K | L | M | N | O | P | Q | R | S | T | U | V | W | X | Y | Z |
|---|---|---|---|---|---|---|---|---|---|---|---|---|---|---|---|---|---|---|---|---|---|---|---|---|---|---|
| Substitute: | W | _ | K | _ | _ | _ | _ | _ | E | _ | _ | _ | T | _ | N | _ | _ | P | _ | _ | _ | _ | M | _ | _ | _ |

Name ______________________ Date __________ Period __________

# 1-78. OPPOSITES ATTRACT

Match each word from the Word Bank with its opposite from the words numbered 1–16. Write the correct number next to its corresponding letter in the Magic Square. If your answers are correct, each column and row in the Magic Square will add up to the same number. Use your dictionary if necessary.

**WORD BANK**

| | | | |
|---|---|---|---|
| A. chaos | E. ennui | I. huge | M. poverty |
| B. placid | F. rigid | J. torrid | N. improvise |
| C. fallow | G. extricate | K. caustic | O. conceal |
| D. flaccid | H. candid | L. blithe | P. circumspect |

1. secretive
2. wealth
3. turbulent
4. soothing
5. frigid
6. productive
7. careless
8. excitement
9. expose
10. flexible
11. diminutive
12. firm
13. order
14. dejected
15. entrap
16. plan

| | | | |
|---|---|---|---|
| A | B | C | D |
| E | F | G | H |
| I | J | K | L |
| M | N | O | P |

Each row and column adds up to this number: ________

Name ______________________ Date __________ Period __________

# 1-79. SPANNING THE ALPHABET

The answers to these 26 questions are as easy as ABC, relatively speaking. Each answer starts with a different letter of the alphabet. Write your answers in the appropriate places within the puzzle.

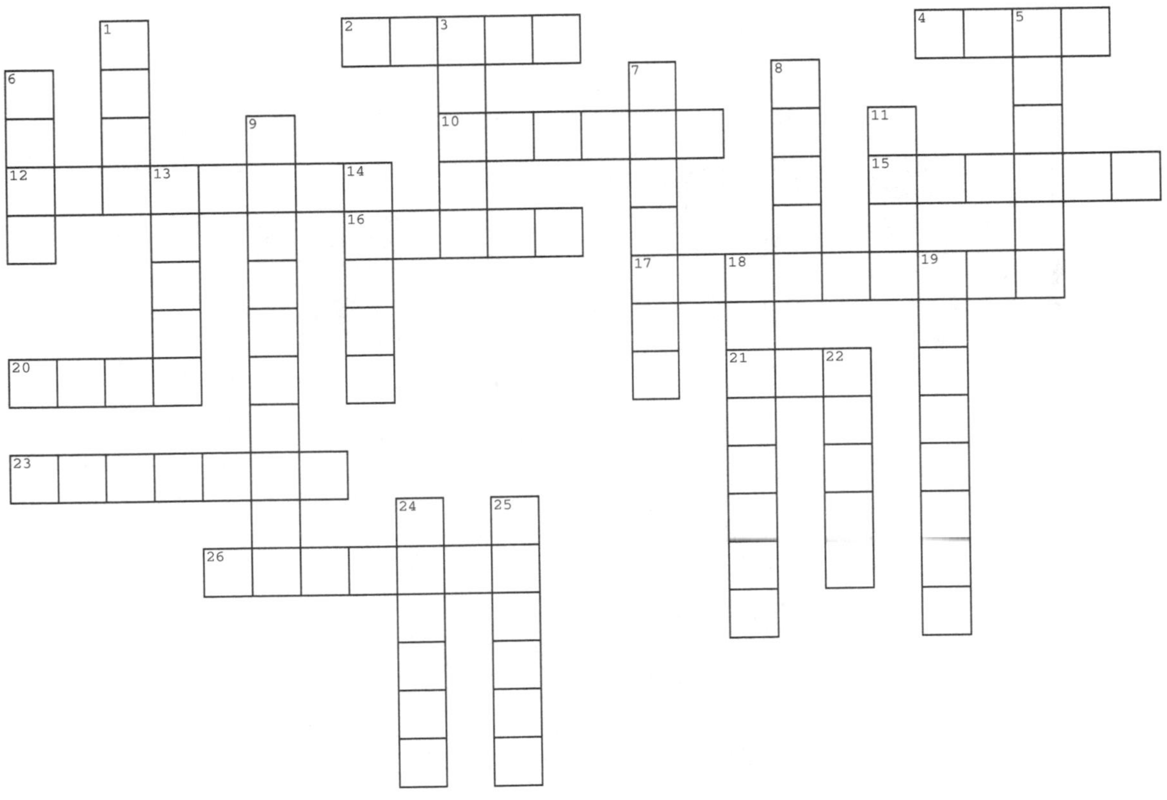



**ACROSS**

2. lure
4. praise
10. not planned
12. a starlike sign
15. risk or peril
16. wanderer
17. goal
20. wharf
21. to annoy or irritate
23. infectious disease
26. Jewish school

**DOWN**

1. tightly stretched
3. to hit and rebound
5. sophisticated
6. prejudice
7. long, narrow boat
8. a period of twenty years
9. opposite of literal
11. to stimulate one's appetite
13. dark or black
14. talent
18. immature or childish
19. sovereign
22. chemical element
24. fastening device
25. pale

Name ______________________________ Date __________ Period __________

# 1-80. TEAMS OF THREE

Based on their definitions, the 30 words in this word-find puzzle can be organized into ten groups of three members each. The listed words are found backward, forward, diagonally, and vertically. At the bottom of this sheet, write the ten groups. Discuss the answers with your classmates.

```
C S A M D Y Z L F X M H G C F C D S V R F F T K
L C P S L W W A F D G A K O S B Y E G E L V W Q
V W F S Y R I D S T I G S N M M J L C F N P T T
Y T I P Y L T S A H G M Q T R E P X E L O X B S
W R E Z R C U Y J O E K V E E L W K V E I R Z W
G G R W A O R M Y U V L S N L R P X P C S N T V
M F C B E R H E V G P K T D Q H F N L T S S E M
B I E D R X D Q M H G W R E F U G E B I A T G R
Z G I X D R I U H T Z X F L R F U S W V P Q L Q
K H G P A C F V O F J L E T Q R D R D E M T O V
V T J H Q M F Y D U N G R T C T X O C V O F O R
N Y D X K M I V N L S C O A Q J B W Z I C J M T
J Q S D R B C F G C Y T C B Q K Z H J S W D Y K
L K R C L T U J M G P N I B F V F N C N R W R M
W Q W Y W N L P F T S J O S K T R Z N E W K Y D
G N F J L X T R K M M J U H G K L W D P L X Q X
X D B N F W X B Z Z G Y S F L M K H Z Z Z K D Q
```

| | | | | |
|---|---|---|---|---|
| ARDUOUS | DECLINE | FEROCIOUS | HARD | REFLECTIVE |
| ASYLUM | DIFFICULT | FIERCE | HIDEOUS | REFUGE |
| BATTLE | DIM | FIGHT | MASTER | SHELTER |
| COMPASSION | DREARY | GHASTLY | MERCY | THOUGHTFUL |
| CONTEND | EXPERT | GLOOMY | PENSIVE | WIZARD |
| CRUEL | FAIL | GRISLY | PITY | WORSEN |

Name ______________________ Date __________ Period __________

# 1-81. CONNECTING THE PREFIX AND THE ROOT

Listed below are 25 roots and prefixes, along with their meanings. Use the roots and prefixes in the box to complete each word.

1. ab _ _ _ _ _(away from)
2. amb_ _ _ _ _ _ _ (to walk)
3. ante_ _ _ _ _ _ _ (before)
4. _ _ _ archy (ruler)
5. bene_ _ _ (good)
6. bio_ _ _ _ _ _ _ (life)
7. chron_ _ _ _ _ (time)
8. dem_ _ _ _ _ _ _ (people)
9. dic _ _ _ (to speak)
10. err_ _ _ _ _ (to wander)
11. _ _flect (to bend)
12. _ _ _gress (to move)
13. hyper_ _ _ _ _ _ _ (over)
14. hypo_ _ _ _ _ _ _ (under)
15. mal_ _ _ _ _ _ _ _ _ (bad)
16. nov_ _ _ (new)
17. ped_ _ _ _ _ _ _ _ (foot)
18. port_ _ _ _ _ _ (to carry)
19. pro_ _ _ _ _ (much)
20. psych_ _ _ _ _ _ (mind)
21. retro_ _ _ _ _ _ _ (behind)
22. se_ _ _ _ _ _ _ (apart)
23. seq_ _ _ _ _ (to follow)
24. _ _vert (to turn)
25. vid_ _ (to see)



| | | | | |
|---|---|---|---|---|
| pro | in | parate | ulance | uence |
| cedent | tion | dermic | eo | function |
| ology | ice | estrian | active | lific |
| rocket | graphy | icle | atic | ocracy |
| sence | fit | folio | mon | de |

Name ______________________ Date __________ Period __________

# 1-82. YOU : WINNER

Match each word from the Word Bank below with its correct analogy beneath the Word Bank. Insert the correct number next to its appropriate matching number within the Magic Square. When your answers are correct, each column and row will add up to the same.

| | | |
|---|---|---|
| A. measure | G. beginning | M. construct |
| B. duchess | H. galaxy | N. weather |
| C. introduction | I. aquatic | O. trunk |
| D. heart | J. malevolent | P. paragraph |
| E. baseball | K. desert | |
| F. rich | L. adverb | |

1. meteorologist : weather as botanist : plants
2. ____________ : end as alpha : omega
3. closely : ____________ as architect : noun
4. ruler : ____________ as watch : time
5. dolphin : ocean as camel : ____________
6. king : queen as duke : ____________
7. raze : demolish as raise : ____________
8. star : ____________ as island : archipelago
9. quarter : football as inning : ____________
10. sentences : ____________ as scenes : act
11. postscript : end as ____________ : beginning
12. beneficent : good as ____________ : evil
13. cardiac : ____________ as vascular : vein
14. horse : terrestrial as whale : ____________
15. affluent : ____________ as indigent : poor
16. ____________ : tree as torso : human

| | | | |
|---|---|---|---|
| A | B | C | D |
| E | F | G | H |
| I | J | K | L |
| M | N = 1 | O | P |

Name ______________________ Date __________ Period __________

# 1-83. START WITH A VOWEL

Each answer begins with a vowel. Write your answers in the appropriate places within the crossword puzzle.

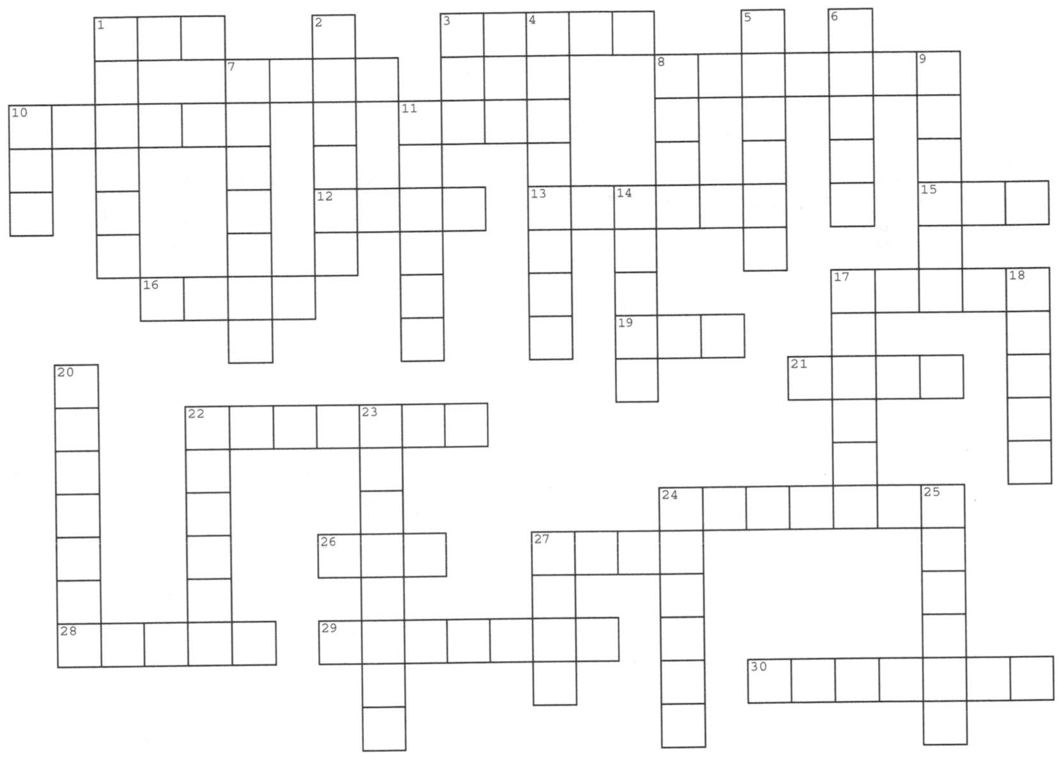



## ACROSS

1. opposite of even
3. large body of water
7. not pretty
8. see
10. one of the four seasons
11. an arm bone
12. wicked
13. planet
15. inquire
16. one of fifty
17. Greek alphabet's final letter
19. not well
21. bit of news or information
22. distress
24. to blow full with air
26. a sphere
27. tiny particle
28. opposite of full
29. to select for an office
30. highest degree

## DOWN

1. choice
2. nine plus two
3. he gives a hoot
4. to make empty
5. to help
6. opposite of rural
7. odd
8. sign
9. to breathe air out
10. Noah's home for awhile
11. joined
14. relating to sound
17. Canada's capital
18. scent
20. to make better
22. a month
23. brave
24. to bring in from the outside
25. tooth's covering
27. a relative

Name ______________________ Date __________ Period __________

# 1-84. SOMETHING IN COMMON

This crossword puzzle will test your ability to think in specifics. The clues are general, but the answers are specific. Several of the clues repeat themselves. For instance, there are three clues that read "type of vehicle." Thus, you will be asked to identify three different types of vehicle. Write your answers in the appropriate places within the puzzle.

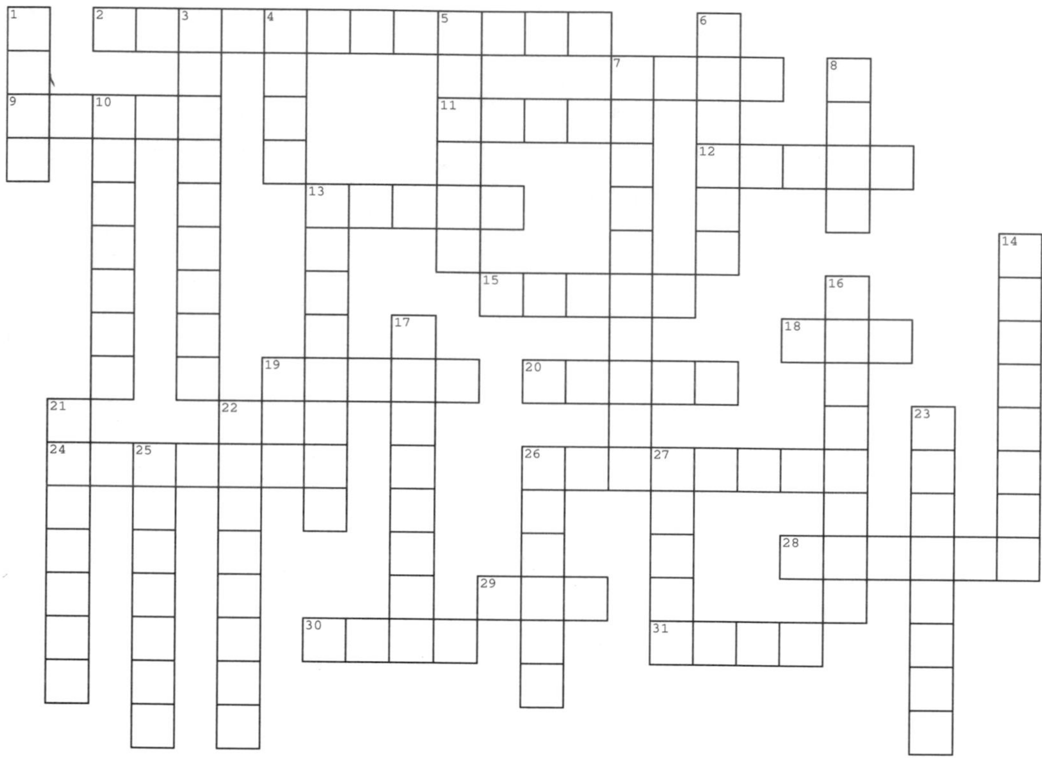



**ACROSS**

2. punctuation term (2 words)
7. musical term
9. horseracing term
11. computer term
12. part of a book
13. part of a boat
15. part of a bicycle
18. part of a boat
19. part of a bicycle
20. land formation
24. military rank
26. musical term
28. land formation
29. type of vehicle
30. type of vehicle
31. musical term

**DOWN**

1. punctuation term
3. part of a dictionary entry
4. part of a bicycle
5. computer term
6. punctuation term
7. part of a dictionary entry
8. part of a boat
10. synonym for worker
13. military rank
14. part of a book
16. military rank
17. computer term
21. horseracing term
22. type of vehicle
23. synonym for worker
25. horseracing term
26. architecture term
27. punctuation term

Name ______________________ Date __________ Period __________

# 1-85. END WHERE YOU BEGAN

The idea of this puzzle is rather elementary. Whatever letter starts the answer, the same letter ends the answer. It is that simple! Write your answers in the appropriate places. Good luck.

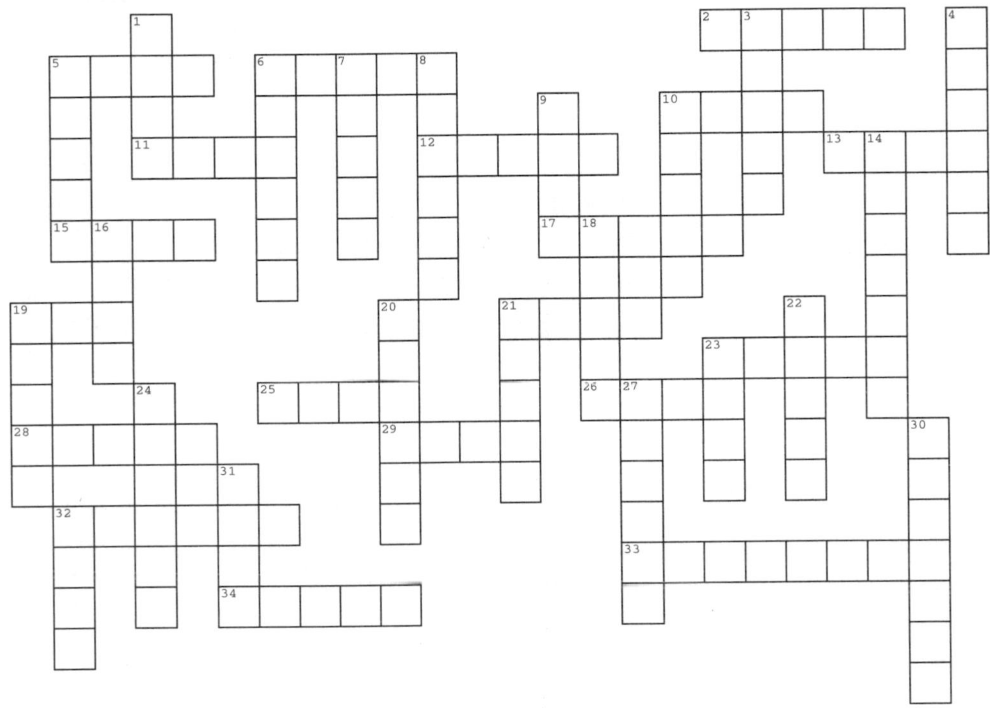



**ACROSS**

2. soft, light down
5. alcoholic liquor
6. deceased husband's wife
10. foot and leg movement
11. sign type
12. even
13. rude talk
15. bell's sound
17. detection system
19. Adam's mate
21. support or hold up
23. pay for another
25. loud noise
26. part of an opera
28. belief
29. injure severely
32. excitement
33. move to another country
34. book advertisement

**DOWN**

1. time of day
3. nearby
4. cold American state
5. form of the verb *to go*
6. a real pane
7. anticipate with anxiety
8. tree
9. opposite of front
10. Eskimo canoe
14. Canadian province
16. specific cookie
18. scent
19. the best
20. whisper
21. on the heavy side
22. famous company
23. tight
24. fireplace floor
27. boat part used for steering
30. nature
31. sharp point on a fishhook
32. not low

Name ______________________ Date __________ Period __________

# 1-86. X MARKS THE SPOT

Each of the 30 words in this puzzle contains the letter X. The first letter, the last letter, and number of letters in each word are found beneath the puzzle. Words are placed backward, forward, diagonally, and vertically. Circle the 30 words containing the letter X and then write each word in its appropriate place below the puzzle.

```
V F R K G L X Z Z L Z Y T Z M K W T S D G S V Q
G S B J D V D S M F F S G T K F B H X M J T H B
L R U F K B Z E T H H C L E N Z F E K R S C V S
Y E Q O L Y T R M T R A X J X H P X S T G A K Y
D H P S I C N R E U N V X H N T D P V T N R P S
L P C G Q X R B X D H B E I E V I A X X Y T I H
S A X O P H O N E T U X E D O X E N E G Y X O H
Q R X E Y G A N L X I X E L E M I D C R A E A P
H G R Z L P S N O T L D V R G H N L U T D Y H W
T O X I C F Z M X J T F M L P I J X E E H X B G
T C D Y K X C U J I F R T S C Y U D Z H Q B B M
X I H M G V R C D Y E N V T D L M I K D J R R X
B X F Y C C J L Z Z J T L T S I M R E D I X A T
F E X B F S S D P B Q J Y J H I J V S B C C P K
N L D G F R F D W H B Z R T X W X T K S P V P X
K V K L V G F F P X S K F A L Q B Y S V H Q W B
N D R W N H J V T T W G M X N L L P D S V Q N Q
```

| | | |
|---|---|---|
| A________S (4) | F________X (4) | O________N (6) |
| A________M (5) | H________X (3) | R________X (3) |
| A________Y (7) | H________X (5) | R________X (5) |
| B________M (5) | I________X (5) | S________X (4) |
| C________X (4) | L________X (3) | S________X (6) |
| E________T (4) | L________Y (6) | S________E (9) |
| E________D (6) | L________R (13) | T________C (5) |
| E________T (6) | M________E (8) | T________O (6) |
| E________T (7) | N________S (7) | T________T (11) |
| E________T (7) | O________N (4) | W________X (3) |

Name ______________________ Date __________ Period __________

# 1-87. SMALL'S SYNONYMS

Twenty synonyms for the word *small* are in cryptic form below. Identify the letters that were substituted in the original word and write them in the appropriate spaces. In this cryptic, every time the letter *W* appears, it has been substituted for the letter *M*, the letter *K* has been substituted for the letter *L*, and the letter *Y* has been substituted for the letter *I*. A list of letters (with a clue or two) is at the bottom of this sheet.

1. WYHLBGLKF = _ _ _ _ _ _ _ _ _ _
2. WYHYDULJF = _ _ _ _ _ _ _ _ _ _
3. LHYWEZJUDHU = _ _ _ _ _ _ _ _ _ _ _ _ _
4. EFUYUF = _ _ _ _ _ _
5. ELHQ = _ _ _ _
6. UMYH = _ _ _ _
7. RJYFN = _ _ _ _ _
8. UJYNKYHP = _ _ _ _ _ _ _ _
9. JFILGFI = _ _ _ _ _ _ _
10. WYHZJ = _ _ _ _ _
11. BULHUFI = _ _ _ _ _ _ _
12. WHYLUF = _ _ _ _ _ _
13. KYUUKF = _ _ _ _ _ _
14. BEDJF = _ _ _ _ _
15. GZWEDGU = _ _ _ _ _ _ _
16. KYWYUFI = _ _ _ _ _ _ _
17. BKYPMU = _ _ _ _ _ _
18. BKFHIFJ = _ _ _ _ _ _ _
19. YHBYPHYNYGDHU = _ _ _ _ _ _ _ _ _ _ _ _ _
20. YHGZHBFALFHUYDK = _ _ _ _ _ _ _ _ _ _ _ _ _ _ _

*Letter Substitution Code Used:*

| Letter: | A | B | C | D | E | F | G | H | I | J | K | L | M | N | O | P | Q | R | S | T | U | V | W | X | Y | Z |
|---|---|---|---|---|---|---|---|---|---|---|---|---|---|---|---|---|---|---|---|---|---|---|---|---|---|---|
| Substitute: | _ | _ | _ | I | _ | N | P | _ | Y | _ | _ | K | W | _ | _ | E | _ | _ | _ | U | _ | S | T | _ | _ | _ |

Name ______________________________ Date __________ Period __________

# 1-88. SYNONYMS FOR BIG

Thirty synonyms for the word *big* are hidden in this word-find puzzle. The words have been placed backward, forward, diagonally, and vertically. The first letter, last letter, and the number of letters in each word are given to you. Circle the 30 synonyms and then complete the spelling of the words on the appropriate lines.

```
V Q S L N N Q Y T Q E N R Y T P N H V L S G S V
X A D M Z O Q T V X F X K G V A U L J U G A I V
W N S C X G T N T S S L G J J G E A O F I R G Q
I T Y T H G I E W S U O D N E M E R T R G G N D
M M N G R S N N W B O O K E G M E G G E A A I B
P L M A F S C I S O M M I S T N I E R W N N F G
O K B E I W I M C U R P B G E A I N J O T T I Y
R D Q V N G T O O S O T O G I S L K E P I U C F
T G E I Q S S R L M N R H N C D O F L N C A A W
A T B S T C E P O B E N T Y D Y O I N U T N N L
N Y N S D D J V S Y S Q L S J E L R D I H K T Y
T W D A Y M A M S V K L L W N H R P P N V P Y Y
P S W M X Z M C A L C S L Y Y O Y O W B A Q S V
P T X R J H K R L C H V D Q Z N M K U K T R T D
P Y K Z G M T F X N N C N Z B C C J K S V Z G M
C H Q G H Y Y Y Q K Q L Z T S V H H G P H V N P
C O N S E Q U E N T I A L D Y Y Y N R R K K V L
```

B__________Y (5)
C__________L (8)
C__________L (13)
E__________T (7)
E__________S (8)
E__________E (9)
G__________T (5)
G__________T (5)
G__________S (8)
G__________C (8)

G__________E (9)
G__________N (10)
H__________E (4)
H__________G (7)
I__________E (7)
I__________D (8)
I__________E (9)
L__________E (5)
M__________E (7)
M__________C (8)

M__________S (9)
N__________Y (10)
P__________L (8)
P__________S (9)
P__________T (9)
P__________S (10)
S__________T (11)
T__________S (10)
V__________T (4)
W__________Y (7)

Name ______________________ Date __________ Period __________

# 1-89. SYNONYMS FOR TALK

Twenty synonyms for the word *talk* are in cryptic form below. Identify the letters that were substituted in the original word and write them in the appropriate spaces. In this cryptic, every time the letter *F* appears, it has been substituted for the letter *E*, and the letter *T* has been substituted for the letter *S*. A list of letters (with a clue or two) is at the bottom of this sheet.

1. AFKDGYF = _ _ _ _ _ _ _
2. USSYFTT = _ _ _ _ _ _ _
3. UYDPKGAUDF = _ _ _ _ _ _ _ _ _ _
4. TFYXCVPNF = _ _ _ _ _ _ _ _ _
5. JUYAFQ = _ _ _ _ _ _
6. WCTTPJ = _ _ _ _ _ _
7. KCVTGAD = _ _ _ _ _ _ _
8. JYFUKE = _ _ _ _ _ _
9. KCXXGVPKUDF = _ _ _ _ _ _ _ _ _ _ _
10. CYUDF = _ _ _ _ _
11. JCVDPLPKUDF = _ _ _ _ _ _ _ _ _ _ _
12. TJFUR = _ _ _ _ _
13. FHJYFTT = _ _ _ _ _ _ _
14. DFAA = _ _ _ _
15. KEUDDFY = _ _ _ _ _ _ _
16. KCVLFY = _ _ _ _ _ _
17. JYCKAUPX = _ _ _ _ _ _ _ _
18. SFKAUPX = _ _ _ _ _ _ _
19. TUQ = _ _ _
20. KEUD = _ _ _ _

*Letter Substitution Code Used:*

| Letter: | A | B | C | D | E | F | G | H | I | J | K | L | M | N | O | P | Q | R | S | T | U | V | W | X | Y | Z |
|---|---|---|---|---|---|---|---|---|---|---|---|---|---|---|---|---|---|---|---|---|---|---|---|---|---|---|
| Substitute: | _ | I | _ | _ | F | L | _ | E | _ | _ | _ | A | _ | _ | _ | J | _ | _ | T | _ | _ | _ | O | _ | _ | N |

Name ______________________ Date __________ Period __________

# 1-90. THREE'S COMPANY

Eleven words are the only clues in this crossword puzzle that has 33 answers. Each of these eleven words has three answers. Thus, the word *lampoon* is used as a clue three times and has three different answers. Write your answers in the appropriate places within the puzzle.

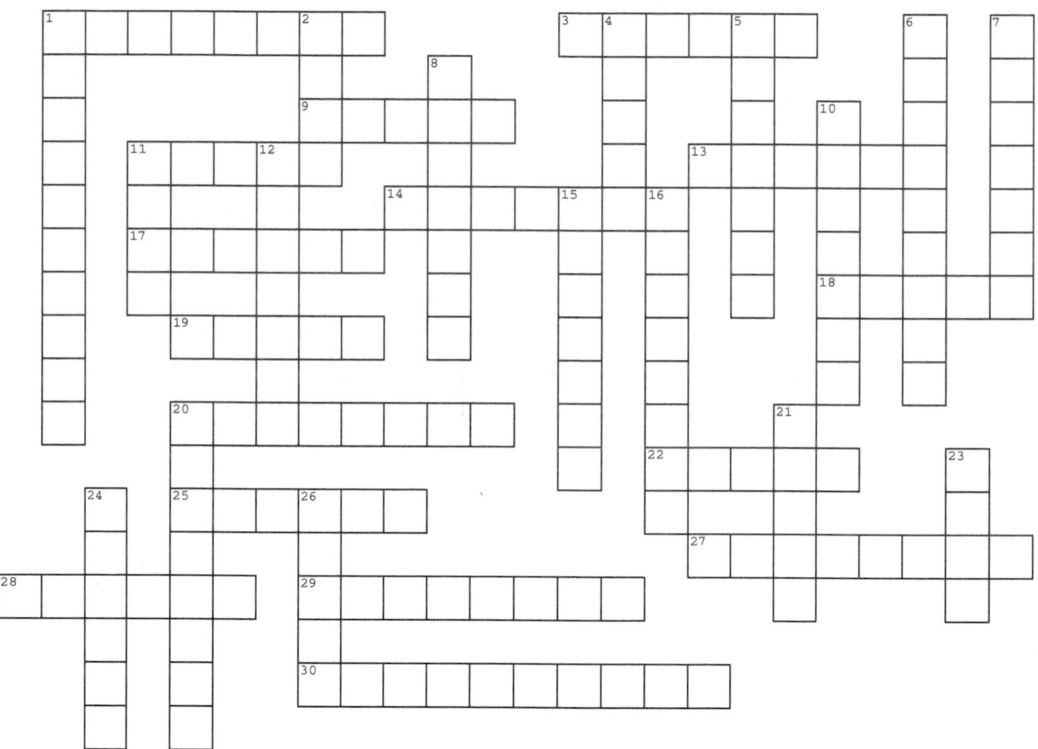



**ACROSS**

1. lampoon
3. singular
9. majestic
11. bogus
13. guarantee
14. propose
17. majestic
18. tempt
19. perfect
20. lampoon
22. faithful
25. lampoon
27. bogus
28. perfect
29. perfect
30. singular

**DOWN**

1. senseless
2. tempt
4. majestic
5. obscure
6. obscure
7. guarantee
8. guarantee
10. senseless
11. bogus
12. propose
15. senseless
16. faithful
20. singular
21. obscure
23. faithful
24. tempt
26. propose

# ANSWER KEY

## 1-1. FINDING FIVE

| | | | | |
|---|---|---|---|---|
| 1. adj | 6. n | 11. con | 16. con | 21. adv |
| 2. con | 7. adv | 12. adj | 17. v | 22. v |
| 3. con | 8. adj | 13. v | 18. n | 23. adj |
| 4. v | 9. n | 14. adv | 19. adj | 24. adv |
| 5. v | 10. n | 15. n | 20. con | 25. adv |

## 1-2. PARTS OF SPEECH

| | | |
|---|---|---|
| 1. noun | 6. verb | 11. adjective |
| 2. verb | 7. noun | 12. verb |
| 3. verb | 8. adverb | 13. noun |
| 4. adjective | 9. preposition | 14. verb |
| 5. noun | 10. adjective | 15. noun |

## 1-3. PARTS-OF-SPEECH VERSATILITY CHECK

1. catastrophe, creed, ministry
2. catalog, crow, note
3. learn, ponder
4. economy
5. academic, gorgeous, prudent
6. truthfully
7. only
8. into
9. motor (noun, verb, adjective); swell (noun, verb, adjective); taboo (noun, verb, adjective); vacuum (noun, verb, adjective)
10. on

Sentences will vary.

## 1-4. PARTS OF SPEECH RACE

***Group One:***

fossil: (2) noun, adjective
raise: (2) noun, verb
run: (3) noun, verb, adjective
low: (4) noun, verb, adjective, adverb
go: (3) noun, verb, adjective
**Total:** 14

### *Group Two*

ego: (1) noun
case: (2) noun, verb
down: (5) noun, verb, adjective, adverb, preposition
table: (3) noun, verb, adjective
high: (3) noun, adjective, adverb
**Total:** 14

### *Group Three*

salt: (3) noun, verb, adjective
right: (5) noun, verb, adjective, adverb, interjection
haul: (2) noun, verb
cast: (2) noun, verb
vent: (2) noun, verb
**Total:** 14

It is a three-way tie!

## 1-5. A VARIETY OF WAYS

Answers will vary. The following are suggestions.

1. (a) He had a bad break in his arm. (b) The runner tried to break the record.
2. (a) The student received a grant of $3,000 for her first year in college. (b) I will grant you permission to go there.
3. (a) My father bought my older brother an iron to use in college. (b) Linda wants to iron things out between you and her. (c) The dictator ruled with an iron fist.
4. (a) Please turn on the overhead light now. (b) I want to light the candles on the birthday cake. (c) A light rain was falling. (d) The package felt light.
5. (a) Tommy arrived at the bus in the nick of time. (b) He said he did not nick the table with the screwdriver.
6. (a) They are members of the now generation. (b) Frankie has to leave now. (c) Now that you have met one another, I will go and prepare the dessert.

## 1-6. EVERYBODY HAS THREE!

| | | |
|---|---|---|
| 1. D | 6. B | 11. E |
| 2. B | 7. C | 12. A |
| 3. C | 8. A | 13. E |
| 4. B | 9. D | 14. A |
| 5. E | 10. D | 15. C |

## 1-7. GETTING TO KNOW THE WHOLE FAMILY

| | | | |
|---|---|---|---|
| 2. barbarism | barbarize | barbaric | barbarically |
| 3. snow (snowiness) | snow | snowy | snowily |
| 4. savor | savor | savored/savory | savorily |
| 5. report | report | reported | reportedly |
| 6. preparedness | prepare | prepared | preparedly |
| 7. friend | befriend | friendly | friendily |
| 8. reservation | reserve | reserved | reservedly |
| 9. freshness | freshen | fresh | freshly |
| 10. agreement | agree | agreeable | agreeably |

## 1-8. PRONOUN PROBLEMS

| | | | |
|---|---|---|---|
| 1. me | 6. she | 11. me | 16. his |
| 2. she | 7. are | 12. themselves | 17. us |
| 3. us | 8. us | 13. who | 18. is |
| 4. herself | 9. she | 14. his | 19. me |
| 5. she | 10. whom | 15. her | 20. he |

## 1-9. CATCH 22

| | | | |
|---|---|---|---|
| 1. 8 | 6. 1/2 | 11. 2 | 16. 1/2 |
| 2. 3 | 7. 1-1/2 | 12. 1 | 17. 12 |
| 3. 1 | 8. 9 | 13. 6 | 18. 7 |
| 4. 4 | 9. 4 | 14. 10 | 19. 1/2 |
| 5. 6 | 10. 7 | 15. 3 | 20. 2 |
| **Total** 22 | **Total** 22 | **Total** 22 | **Total** 22 |

## 1-10. IS IT INEQUAL OR UNEQUAL?

1. **dis-** disavow, disband, discharge, discontent, dishearten
2. **il-** illegal, illegible, illegitimate, illicit, illiterate
3. **im-** immobilize, immovable, impassable, impenitent, impertinent
4. **ir-** irrational, irregular, irrelevant, irreparable, irresolute
5. **non-** nonessential, nonfiction, nonporous, nontaxable, nonusable
6. **un-** unequal, unfair, unfertile, unfortunate, unguarded

## 1-11. PREFIXES THAT NEGATE

| | | |
|---|---|---|
| 1. H | 6. K | 11. L |
| 2. I | 7. F | 12. E |
| 3. J | 8. O | 13. D |
| 4. A | 9. G | 14. M |
| 5. C | 10. B | 15. N |

Words found in the answer column: HIJACK (#1–6), FOG (#7–9), BLED (#10–13). Other possible answers could be HI (#1–2), JACK (#3–6), and LED (#11–13).

## 1-12. TOO MUCH OR TOO LITTLE?

| | | | |
|---|---|---|---|
| 1. warrant | 6. exaggerate | 11. commitment | 16. balloon |
| 2. temperament | 7. myrrh | 12. frightening | 17. foliage |
| 3. collaborate | 8. innate | 13. vacuum | 18. leisure |
| 4. bookkeeper | 9. phosphorous | 14. filament | 19. manual |
| 5. receipt | 10. inferior | 15. preferred | 20. aardvark |

Specific place: Raleigh, North Carolina.

## 1-13. SPELLING YOUR WAY TO THE MOVIE'S TITLE

| | |
|---|---|
| 1. familiar | 9. beginning |
| 2. eligible | 10. recommend |
| 3. despair | 11. occurred |
| 4. hilarious | 12. excellent |
| 5. tomorrow | 13. refusal |
| 6. harass | 14. temperament |
| 7. esteem | 15. illegal |
| 8. forfeit | 16. approval |

Four-word movie title: FATHER OF THE BRIDE

## 1-14. SPELLING IN PARTS

| *Group One* | *Group Two* |
|---|---|
| 1. blinding | 1. complement |
| 2. challenge | 2. effectively |
| 3. circumnavigate | 3. horrendous |

4. friendship
5. gratitude
6. numerical
7. offensive
8. simplicity
9. symphony
10. thunderous

4. illicit
5. mystical
6. mythological
7. persuasive
8. standardized
9. thickness
10. wonderful

## 1-15. MAKING THE UNCLEAR CLEAR

1. all ready, already
2. advice, advise
3. clothes, cloths
4. passed, past
5. hear, here
6. Whether, weather
7. weak, week
8. You're, your
9. their, there, they're
10. to, too
11. principle, principal
12. course, coarse
13. alter, altar
14. plane, plain
15. quite, quiet

## 1-16. ONE OF THEM

Though these answers seem the most appropriate, invite discussion.

1. vowed
2. anachronism
3. tariff
4. impasse
5. novice
6. verdict
7. complied
8. ordinance
9. impresario
10. constituents
11. talented
12. disparaging
13. ominous
14. snubbed
15. incision

## 1-17. AWARDS

1. O—bale
2. S—astronomy
3. C—route
4. A—indolent
5. R—a vendetta
6. E—nadir
7. M—to chafe
8. M—royal
9. Y—catastrophe
10. T—plane
11. O—doubtful
12. N—surpass
13. Y—fiancee
14. G—capitol
15. R—avocation
16. A—meteorologist
17. M—infectious
18. M—principle
19. Y—anxious

These four words are the names of awards: Oscar (movies), Emmy (television), Tony (theater), and Grammy (music).

## 1-18. WHAT'S THE DIFFERENCE?

1. *avid:* eager and enthusiastic
   *fanatical:* unreasonably enthusiastic
2. *concerned:* involved or interested
   *officious:* offering unnecessary advice
3. *continual:* happening over and over again
   *continuous:* unbroken; going on without interruption
4. *credible:* believable
   *credulous:* easily convinced
5. *curt:* brief to the point of rudeness
   *terse:* concise in a polished, smooth way
6. *daring:* fearless
   *reckless:* careless, heedless
7. *disinterested:* not influenced by personal interest
   *indifferent:* showing no partiality or preference
8. *famous:* renowned
   *infamous:* having a bad reputation
9. *firm:* not yielding easily under pressure
   *stubborn:* refusing to yield, obey, or comply
10. *hound:* chase or follow continually; nag
    *pursue:* to strive for; devote oneself to
11. *immoral:* not in conformity with accepted principles of right and wrong behavior
    *amoral:* without moral sense or principles
12. *sarcastic:* caustic and cutting
    *sardonic:* bitterly sneering
13. *stroll:* walk in a leisurely manner
    *strut:* walk in a stiff, swaggering manner
14. *willfully:* doing as one pleases
    *willingly:* readily; voluntarily
15. *wise:* prudent; showing good judgment
    *pedantic:* showing off one's knowledge

## 1-19. FORMING THE WORDS

comprehend
criterion
demographics
disparity
equivocal
homogeneous
impassioned
inadvertent
irrevocable
metamorphosis
parapsychology
partisan
pretentious
reiterate
sophomoric

## 1-20. POSITIVE AND NEGATIVE ADJECTIVES

Answers will vary. The following are suggestions.

a. agile; awkward
b. brilliant; bland
c. caring; crude
d. diligent; drab
e. elegant; erroneous
f. friendly; furtive
g. good; ghastly
h. hearty; horrible
i. illustrious; immature
j. jovial; junky
k. kind; knavish
l. lovely; lonely
m. meaningful; mean
n. nimble; noisome
o. objective; obese
p. pure; poor
q. quaint; questionable
r. rich; rancid
s. sensible; stolen
t. truthful; terrible
u. unbeaten; uninspired
v. valiant; violent
w. wonderful; whiny
y. youthful; yucky
z. zesty; zany

## 1-21. SENSATIONAL WORDS

1. bitter
2. reeky
3. spicy
4. brittle
5. foggy
6. bland
7. creamy
8. tasty
9. lukewarm
10. tart
11. arid
12. oily
13. ugly
14. dry
15. pretty
16. deafening
17. wet
18. aromatic
19. itchy
20. rusty

Four words: brief (#1–5), date (#6–9), tail (#10–13), defects (#14–20)

## 1-22. MAKING SENSE OF ANALOGIES

These are the relationships. Students' analogies will vary

1. A puzzle is cryptic or puzzling.
2. If one is idle, he is not working.
3. To plunder is to steal or ransack.
4. A doodad is trivial or unimportant.
5. Veracity (truth) is the opposite of duplicity (insincerity or deceit).
6. Both words mean a substance can be ignited.
7. Awkward is the opposite of lithe (agile).
8. A tyrant is much the same as a despot.
9. Vice (wickedness) and virtue (goodness) are opposites.

10. To bisect is to cut in half.
11. Postscript comes after the body of the letter.
12. To counsel is to give advice.
13. Deluge (flood) and drought (lack of moisture) are antonyms.
14. Defer (put off) and delay share the same meaning.
15. Ultra- is a prefix that means beyond.
16. Inter- is a prefix that means between.
17. Intro- means within, the opposite of outside.
18. A dilemma is a difficult problem, one that is not easy.
19. If a person is tolerant, he or she is not disrespectful.
20. Friction is the opposite of smoothness.
21. Venus was a goddess known for her beauty, not her ugliness.
22. To be avid is to be eager.
23. Green is the color that symbolizes envy (jealousy).
24. Inferior and superior are antonyms.
25. Arson is the crime of setting fire to property.

## 1-23. KNOCKING DOWN THOSE ANALOGIES!

| | | | |
|---|---|---|---|
| 1. C | 6. R | 11. S | 16. O |
| 2. O | 7. I | 12. A | 17. G |
| 3. M | 8. S | 13. N | 18. I |
| 4. P | 9. O | 14. A | 19. E |
| 5. A | 10. N | 15. L | 20. S |

Two words spelled: COMPARISONS and ANALOGIES

## 1-24. DOUBLING THE SIZE

| **Small** | **Large** | |
|---|---|---|
| confined | capaciuos | infinite |
| cramped | colossal | mammoth |
| diminitive | elephantine | massive |
| minuscule | external | measureless |
| minute | extensive | perpetual |
| narrow | gigantic | prodigious |
| puny | huge | roomy |
| trivial | immense | towering |

## 1-25. TRIPLE THREAT

1. frame
2. leg
3. heart
4. set
5. tooth
6. title
7. bottom
8. face
9. mouth
10. step

## 1-26. WORDS WITH MULTIPLE MEANINGS

1. set
2. drive
3. fall
4. set
5. fall
6. act
7. bed
8. run
9. drive
10. act
11. act
12. bed
13. run
14. fall
15. drive
16. set
17. run
18. set
19. act
20. bed

## 1-27. COME AND JOIN US

1. stubborn
2. rummage
3. valorous
4. fracture
5. tarry
6. recoup
7. augment
8. vogue
9. employment
10. tumult
11. utility
12. wax
13. shrouded
14. spite
15. sustain

## 1-28. GROUPING THE ACTIONS TOGETHER

| | | |
|---|---|---|
| 1 | 6 | 6 |
| 2 | 2 | 1 |
| 5 | 5 | 6 |
| 3 | 5 | 1 |
| 3 | 2 | 1 |
| 3 | 3 | 5 |
| 4 | 4 | 3 |
| 6 | 1 | 2 |
| 4 | 4 | 5 |
| 2 | 6 | 4 |

## 1-29. HAPPY? SAD? CONFUSED?

| Happy | Sad | Confused |
|---|---|---|
| delighted | crushed | baffled |
| elated | dejected | bewildered |
| gratified | depressed | flustered |
| pleased | disheartened | mystified |
| satisfied | downcast | perplexed |
| thrilled | heartbroken | stupefied |
| tickled | unhappy | uncertain |

## 1-30. DICTIONARY DASH

| | | | |
|---|---|---|---|
| 1. B | 6. A | 11. A | 16. B |
| 2. B | 7. A | 12. A | 17. B |
| 3. A | 8. A | 13. B | 18. A |
| 4. B | 9. B | 14. B | 19. A |
| 5. A | 10. B | 15. B | 20. B |

## 1-31. PEOPLE'S CHARACTERISTICS

| | | | |
|---|---|---|---|
| N | N | P | P |
| P | P | P | N |
| P | P | P | P |
| N | N | P | N |
| N | N | P | N |
| N | N | P | |
| P | N | N | |

## 1-32. LANGUAGE CONCISENESS

| | | | |
|---|---|---|---|
| 1. lamp | 6. poster | 11. cloud | 16. mountain |
| 2. Canada | 7. sled | 12. desk | 17. movie |
| 3. mirror | 8. whale | 13. blanket | 18. deodorant |
| 4. sun | 9. smoke | 14. horoscope | 19. harbor |
| 5. tongue | 10. shoulder | 15. needle | 20. monument |

## 1-33. DIS ME!

| | | | |
|---|---|---|---|
| 1. QUE | 6. HAL | 11. ONT | 16. BRI |
| 2. BEC | 7. IFA | 12. REA | 17. TIS |
| 3. VAN | 8. XCA | 13. LED | 18. HCO |
| 4. COU | 9. LGA | 14. MON | 19. LUM |
| 5. VER | 10. RYM | 15. TON | 20. BIA |

Six Canadian cities (in order): Quebec, Vancouver, Halifax, Calgary, Montreal, Edmonton.
Canadian province: British Columbia

## 1-34. IDENTIFYING AND SPELLING THE SYNONYMS

1. (a) gash; (b) slash; (c) lance; (d) slit; (e) sever
2. (a) symbol; (b) insignia; (c) token; (d) badge; (e) totem
3. (a) collect; (b) accumulate; (c) pile; (d) amass; (e) glean
4. (a) fabricate; (b) manufacture; (c) mint; (d) produce; (e) construct
5. (a) vague; (b) unclear; (c) cryptic; (d) indefinite; (e) uncertain
6. (a) caution; (b) care; (c) sense; (d) sagacity; (e) economy

## 1-35. IDENTIFYING AND SPELLING THE ANTONYMS

1. (a) join; (b) unite; (c) link; (d) connect; (e) merge
2. (a) soil; (b) stain; (c) defile; (d) pollute; (e) sully
3. (a) reeky; (b) rank; (c) rancid; (d) smelly; (e) sour
4. (a) irresponsible; (b) dishonest; (c) doubtful; (d) questionable; (e)impeachable
5. (a) improve; (b) better; (c) amend (or emend); (d) repair; (e) rehabilitate

## 1-36. WORD WEALTH

Answers will vary. Here are some suggestions.

1. assign; perform; tend; yodel; acquire; grow
2. brash; inquisitive; materialistic; democratic; flimsy; long
3. radio; grill; iris; foot; pretzel; hill
4. patiently; measurably; demandingly; stoically; earnestly; jokingly
5. yourself; hers; mine; ourselves; them; its
6. mechanic; doctor; teacher; plumber; artist; announcer
7. depressed; antisocial; maladjusted; unproductive; illegal; dreadful
8. great; beneficial; fantastic; wonderful; luscious; grand

## 1-37. FILLING IN THOSE ADVERBS

Answers will vary. The following are suggestions.

1. artistically; artfully
2. belatedly; begrudgingly
3. brilliantly; brightly
4. candidly; cantankerously
5. elegantly; elusively
6. flagrantly; fluently
7. gratefully; graciously
8. handsomely; handily
9. manually; maniacally
10. partially; partly
11. peevishly; permanently
12. queerly; quizzically
13. remarkably; regretfully
14. splendidly; sparsely
15. successfully; surely
16. tensely; tenderly
17. thoughtfully; thoroughly
18. unhappily; undoubtedly
19. violently; viciously
20. whimsically; wholly

## 1-38. MYTHOLOGICAL NAMES, DERIVATIONS, AND CURRENT MEANINGS

1. KT
2. CU
3. EQ
4. HR
5. JS
6. LN
7. IV
8. BX
9. FM
10. AP
11. GW
12. DO

## 1-39. BE MORE SPECIFIC

1. S
2. G
3. L
4. A
5. D
6. B
7. T
8. I
9. C
10. K
11. F
12. P
13. E
14. R
15. M
16. Q
17. J
18. O
19. H
20. N

Synonym for happy: GLAD
Sound: TICK
Hairstyle: PERM
Man's first name: JOHN

## 1-40. FROM GENERAL TO SPECIFIC

2. edibles; seafood; clams; steamers
3. transportation vehicle; sea vessel; ship; *USS Constitution*
4. emotion; happiness; elation; euphoria
5. person; lady; woman worker; female crossing guard
6. literature; historical fiction; novel; *The Killer Angels*
7. music; rock and roll; ballad; "Big Bad John"
8. liquid; soft drink; non-cola refreshment; Seven-Up®
9. reading material; magazine weekly magazine; *Time*
10. head wear; man's hat; religious garb; yarmulke

## 1-41. FROM GENERAL TO MORE SPECIFIC TO MOST SPECIFIC

The answers do not have to be in this same order under the **General** column, but the words within each group should be in that order.

| *General* | *More Specific* | *Most Specific* |
|---|---|---|
| leader | president | Abraham Lincoln |
| vehicle | car | Cadillac |
| furniture | bed | twin |
| reading material | book | *To Kill a Mockingbird* |
| road | highway | Route 95 |
| television show | comedy program | *Seinfeld* |
| machine | camera | video camera |
| body part | finger | index finger |
| relative | uncle | Uncle Rick |
| animal | dog | Irish setter |
| body of water | ocean | Pacific |
| food | meat | steak |
| plant | flower | daisy |
| writer | dramatist | Shakespeare |
| exercise | running | sprinting |

## 1-42. IS IT GENERAL, MORE SPECIFIC, OR MOST SPECIFIC?

Invite discussion of these answers. Some answers may be interpreted differently.

1. general
2. general
3. most specific
4. most specific

5. more specific
6. most specific
7. more specific
8. most specific
9. more specific
10. most specific
11. general
12. general
13. most specific
14. most specific
15. more specific
16. more specific
17. more specific
18. most specific
19. most specific
20. general

## 1-43. CAN YOU BE MORE SPECIFIC, PLEASE?

1. DIG: plow, burrow, channel, hoe
2. HAPPY: delighted, elated, thrilled, euphoric
3. HOUSE: cabin, castle, cottage, ranch
4. TRY: venture, endeavor, essay, attempt
5. WIN: triumph, conquer, subdue, vanquish
6. THINK: ponder, reason, reflect, meditate
7. SMELLY: reeky, foul, rancid, putrid
8. LOOK: examine, review, scan, inspect
9. SAD: gloomy, depressed, dejected, downcast
10. FAMOUS: renowned, celebrated, prominent, noted

## 1-44. UNSCRAMBLING THE SPECIFICS

**Animals:** kangaroo, giraffe, elephant, tiger
**Body Parts:** elbow, heart, ankle, neck
**Occupations:** teacher, mason, architect, writer
**Land Formations:** desert, valley, mountain, ravine
**Reading Material:** novel, magazine, journal, newspaper
**School Subjects:** English, math, science, history
**Sports:** volleyball, soccer, tennis, football
**Vehicles:** sled, automobile, train, truck

## 1-45. FISHING AROUND FOR SOME CORRECT ANSWERS

**Fashion Statements:** stylish, elegant, refined, suave; NETS
**Friends:** chum, confidant, crony, sidekick; HOOK
**How We Walk:** stride, stroll, saunter, amble; BAIT

**Moods:** elation, euphoria, happiness, rapture; LINE
**Quarrels:** dispute, breakout, squabble, wrangle; POLE
**Airborne Objects:** cloud, dirigible, kite, rocket; DOCK

## 1-46. LET'S GET A MORE EXACT WORD

Answers will vary. The following are suggested verbs.

1. hurl, sling, toss, cast, fling, pitch
2. beam, grin, laugh, smirk, snicker
3. communicate, converse, rap, gossip, confer, consult
4. discern, sight, spot, visualize, notice, observe, understand
5. scent, sniff, snuff, inhale, detect
6. savor, relish
7. bake, roast, broil, fry, simmer, steam, stew
8. feel, palm, finger, stroke, caress
9. labor, toil, sweat, operate, run, strive
10. treat, engross, charm, please, host, welcome
11. peruse, study, review, scrutinize, interpret, scan, skim
12. giggle, snicker, titter
13. ponder, ruminate, conceive, imagine, meditate, deliberate, reflect
14. spring, leap, hop, bound, pounce
15. slash, slice, slit, gash, tear, dissect

## 1-47. LET'S TALK IT UP

1. to talk; to interact socially
2. to seek an opinion from
3. to consider and argue the pros and cons of
4. to keep in mind or take into account
5. to engage in idle talk and rumor
6. to tell the story of; to narrate
7. to talk foolishly or too much
8. to engage in light, familiar, informal talk
9. to speak directly to
10. to make clearly known
11. to counsel
12. to give knowledge of something to
13. to release an opinion or mood

14. to free from ignorance, prejudice, or superstition
15. to depart temporarily from the main subject

Paragraphs will vary.

## 1-48. USAGE SITUATIONS

1. amount
2. childish
3. themselves
4. effect
5. than
6. personnel
7. well
8. irritate
9. compliment
10. good
11. formerly
12. well
13. criteria
14. uninterested
15. eminent
16. differs from
17. conscious
18. number
19. among
20. capital
21. loose
22. council
23. counsel

The quotation: TIME AND TIDE WAIT FOR NO ONE

## 1-49. NOTING THE DIFFERENCE

### *Group One: ROADS*

(a) *boulevard:* a broad, well-made street often lined with trees
(b) *expressway:* a divided highway for through traffic with overpasses and underpasses
(c) *rotary:* a traffic circle

### *Group Two: INSTRUCTORS*

(a) *teacher:* one who teaches as a profession
(b) *professor:* a college or university teacher of the highest rank usually in a specific field
(c) *instructor:* a person who teaches; a college teacher ranking below an assistant professor

### *Group Three: PERSONALITY DESCRIBERS*

(a) *proud:* having a proper respect for oneself
(b) *contented:* having no desire for something more; satisfied
(c) *conceited:* having an exaggerated opinion of oneself

### *Group Four: ACTIONS*

(a) *tease:* to annoy by persistent mocking or poking fun
(b) *harass:* to trouble, worry, or torment repeatedly
(c) *torment:* to cause great physical pain or mental suffering
(d) *pester:* to annoy constantly with petty irritations

***Group Five: HUMORISTS***

(a) *clown:* a performer who entertains by antics, jokes, and/or tricks
(b) *jokester:* a person who says things to provoke laughter
(c) *lampooner:* a person who uses satirical writing to attack or ridicule

## 1-50. WHEN DO WE JOG? WHEN DO WE SPRINT?

1. guffaw
2. sprint
3. ruin
4. pierce
5. peruse
6. idolize
7. coerce
8. hurl
9. riot
10. ogle
11. conflagration
12. minuscule
13. hilarious
14. frigid
15. torrid
16. obese
17. obnoxious
18. flaunt
19. finicky
20. wallop

## 1-51. CLOSE...BUT DIFFERENT

1. S
2. T
3. E
4. P
5. P
6. E
7. T
8. U
9. N
10. D
11. R
12. A
13. P
14. L
15. A
16. I
17. N

Three land formations: STEPPE, TUNDRA, PLAIN

## 1-52. THERE IS A DIFFERENCE

1. number
2. annoyed
3. celery
4. allusion
5. than
6. sensory
7. famous
8. regardless
9. among
10. themselves
11. amount
12. frustration

Shade is a <u>nuance</u>; man's first name is <u>Alan</u>; piece of furniture is <u>sofa</u>; quantity of paper is <u>ream</u>; feeling is <u>emotion</u>

## 1-53. POSITIVE AND NEGATIVE CONNOTATIONS

1. af
2. fi
3. rm
4. at
5. iv
6. ec
7. er
8. ta
9. in
10. co
11. nt
12. ra

13. di
14. ct
15. or
16. ya
17. nn
18. ul
19. li
20. ng

Two synonyms for positive: affirmative and certain
Two synonyms for negative: contradictory and annulling

## 1-54. THE GOOD AND THE BAD

1. blare
2. spastic
3. strangle
4. bland
5. guffaw
6. eyesore
7. ludicrous
8. hovel
9. ornate
10. indigent
11. failure
12. deluge
13. grimace
14. chaotic
15. arrogant
16. dearth
17. trudge
18. coarse
19. fallow
20. narrow-minded

## 1-55. COMPLETING THE QUOTE

1. consent
2. elders
3. abuse
4. lies
5. defect
6. geography
7. time
8. vices
9. generous
10. refreshment
11. imitation
12. fate

## 1-56. DESCRIBING A CHARACTER

Answers will vary.

## 1-57. MATCHING THE MASTERS

1. spirited-looking; curly; parted; oval; eyebrows
2. dark-skinned; dress; manners; squire; slovenly; amiss; erect; handsome
3. white; red; shoes; stripes; hair; leapt; chasing; street
4. student; eyes; cold; deep; used
5. however; simple; moreover; obedient; husband

## 1-58. ADJECTIVES RELATED TO OUR SENSES

Answers will vary.

## 1-59. ILLUSTRATING A PERSON'S CHARACTERISTICS

Answers will vary.

## 1-60. MOOD INDICATORS

Answer will vary. The following are suggestions.

1. uncertain
2. agreeing with
3. loud laughing
4. showed displeasure
5. not believing easily
6. cold
7. trying hard to hear
8. trying hard to hear
9. could not believe
10. working hard; concentrating on his task
11. showed interest; found it hard to believe
12. nervousness
13. showing extreme distaste for
14. prepared herself for the hard task
15. sneakily

## 1-61. THE RESPONSE

Sentences will vary. The following are the definitions.

1. having conflicting feelings
2. rough and abrupt; curt
3. fair; honest; frank
4. biting; sharp
5. placating; bringing two opposing views together
6. patronizing; stooping
7. repentant; sorrowful for an offense
8. tending to find fault; censorious
9. belittling; discrediting
10. overflowing with enthusiam
11. glib; impertinent
12. showing kindness and courtesy; merciful
13. forward; pert; peevish
14. without deceit; honest
15. shallow

## 1-62. USING MORE SPECIFIC VERBS

1. collapsed
2. scraped
3. preached
4. trudged
5. sprinted
6. scrubbed
7. thrashed
8. harmonized
9. probed
10. snickered
11. decoded
12. recalled
13. loathed
14. nudged
15. calculated

## 1-63. DESCRIBING YOUR SURROUNDINGS

Answers will vary.

## 1-64. EXPRESSING YOURSELF THROUGH CLOTHING

1. carefully
2. hidden
3. under control
4. salute or congratulate
5. afraid
6. achievement
7. is the boss
8. member of the religious (clergy)
9. does a variety of things
10. indirect veto by the president
11. in a relaxed way
12. be formal
13. elegant or very formal occasion
14. suit to express grief
15. talk nonsense
16. in another's position
17. strictly confidential
18. the situation is reversed for the persons involved
19. the source of the problem
20. to take one's place

## 1-65. DON'T GET HYPER, BIG CHEESE!

| *Word* | *Informal* | *Slang* |
|---|---|---|
| daze | bowl over | blow one away |
| entangle | suck in | foul up |
| evade | shake off | beat the rap |
| exaggerate | pile it on | shoot the bull |
| finish | get out from under | knock off |
| horrify | turn one's stomach | gross out |
| leader | kingpin | big cheese |
| mislead | throw a curve | snooker |
| nervous | hyper | antsy |
| news | info | dope |
| pay | chip in | dish out |

| | | |
|---|---|---|
| prepare | prep | psych oneself up |
| punch | wallop | conk |
| rant | fly off | shoot off one's mouth |
| shout | holler | belt out |

## 1-66. EXPRESSING YOURSELF WITH EXPRESSIONS

1. R
2. S
3. K
4. N
5. L
6. J
7. G
8. A
9. T
10. B
11. H
12. F
13. D
14. Q
15. C
16. E
17. O
18. M
19. P
20. I

## 1-67. EXPRESSIONS USING BODY PARTS

1. ear
2. foot
3. arm; leg
4. mouth
5. tongue
6. leg
7. foot
8. ear
9. tooth; nail
10. head
11. tooth
12. nail
13. eye
14. nose (for hand)
15. nose; face
16. tongue
17. head; shoulders
18. toe
19. legs
20. eye; eye

## 1-68. FIT AS A FIDDLE WITH THESE EXPRESSIONS!

1. achievement
2. guess
3. hinder; hamper
4. comfortable; enviable place
5. earned the money
6. become angry
7. exact; no questions asked
8. stop the warfare; stop the bickering
9. my limit; will not go beyond that point
10. start at the beginning
11. be scolded; be questioned
12. caught in the wrongful act
13. small amount; worthless amount
14. went crazy
15. the unpleasant was imminent
16. weak spot; downfall
17. last minute
18. very different from the norm
19. try to be deceptive; to deceive
20. one who takes the blame for the others

## 1-69. NO MONKEYING AROUND HERE!

1. monkey bars
2. rabbit ears
3. bull session
4. dog days
5. bunny hop
6. cat-o'-nine-tails
7. fox trot
8. bird dog

9. paper tiger
10. crocodile tears
11. pig Latin
12. chicken pox
13. Pony Express
14. goose step
15. pigtail
16. horseshoes
17. kangaroo court
18. snake pit
19. duckpins
20. catwalk

## 1-70. SELECTING THE CORRECT WORD

1. to
2. on
3. on
4. with
5. in
6. to
7. to
8. of
9. to
10. about
11. for
12. to
13. from
14. in
15. by

The five 3-letter words: TOO, WIT, TOT, AFT, FIB

## 1-71. POSITIONING WORDS

1. b
2. a
3. a
4. c
5. a
6. a
7. c
8. b
9. a
10. a
11. c
12. b
13. c
14. a
15. b

The students' sentences will vary.

## 1-72. REMOVING WORDS THAT ARE SUPERFLUOUS

Answers may vary. these are suggestions.

1. I will visit the museum tomorrow.
2. The bus will arrive soon.
3. Jason looked at the bus schedule.
4. Mrs. Chamberlain's students will go on the field trip.
5. The class will spend two hours viewing the exhibits at Boston's Children's Museum.
6. The experienced tour guide will meet the class in the foyer.
7. None of Mrs. Chamberlain's students will forget this outing.
8. Some of the museum's exhibits will be rearranged next month.
9. The museum workers helped many people.
10. The children ate lunch in the cafeteria.
11. All of the students were allowed to roam.

12. The guide talked about the ice of the ancient times.
13. We saw the entire exhibit.
14. She spoke of the philanthropists who support the museum.
15. We asked her about the nomads.

## 1-73. WHEN TOO MANY WORDS ARE TOO MUCH

Answers may vary. These are suggestions.

1. The man was arrested for arson.
2. We needed a thesaurus.
3. The professional singer has a beautiful voice.
4. Do not trespass. (or No trespassing.)
5. The Smith College alumnae donated money.
6. Raymond yelled yesterday.
7. The criminal was accused of theft.
8. The repairman repaired the oil burner.
9. I noticed that the neighborhood patrol officer was very happy.
10. Drinking alcoholic beverages is unhealthy.
11. Mr. Munson, a school bus driver, saw a teenage girl speeding in her car.

## 1-74. ARE YOU A LENGOOL? DO YOU LENGOOL?

Answers will vary.

## 1-75. HELPING OUT

Answers will vary.

## 1-76. PLAYING WITH WORDS

| | | | |
|---|---|---|---|
| 1. D | 6. G | 11. I | 16. C |
| 2. R | 7. P | 12. K | 17. T |
| 3. L | 8. M | 13. B | 18. Q |
| 4. E | 9. N | 14. F | 19. O |
| 5. S | 10. H | 15. A | 20. J |

## 1-77. IF THE HAT FITS

1. MORTARBOARD
2. BEANIE
3. TOQUE
4. TOP HAT
5. TEN GALLON
6. BERET
7. YARMULKE
8. HARD HAT
9. BOWLER
10. CAP
11. DERBY
12. FEDORA
13. NIGHTCAP
14. BIRETTA
15. HELMET
16. SKULLCAP
17. STRAW HAT
18. TURBAN
19. FEZ
20. DUNCE CAP

*Letter substitution code used:*

Letter: A B C D E F G H I J K L M N O P Q R S T U V W X Y Z
Code: W J K X V A Z L E C U G T O N R H P Y B S I M Q F D

## 1-78. OPPOSITES ATTRACT

| A = 13 | B = 3 | C = 6 | D = 12 |
|---|---|---|---|
| E = 8 | F = 10 | G = 15 | H = 1 |
| I − 11 | J = 5 | K = 4 | L = 14 |
| M = 2 | N = 16 | O = 9 | P = 7 |

Each row and column adds up to 34.

## 1-79. SPANNING THE ALPHABET

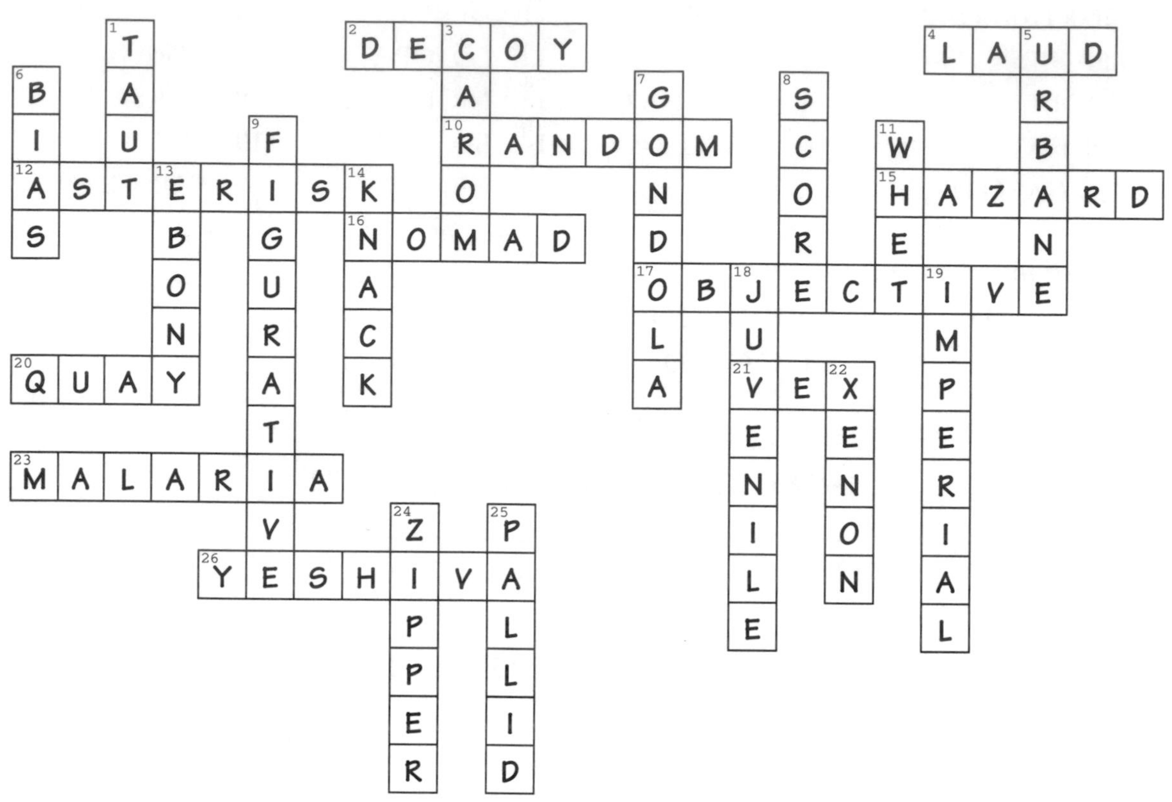

## 1-80. TEAMS OF THREE

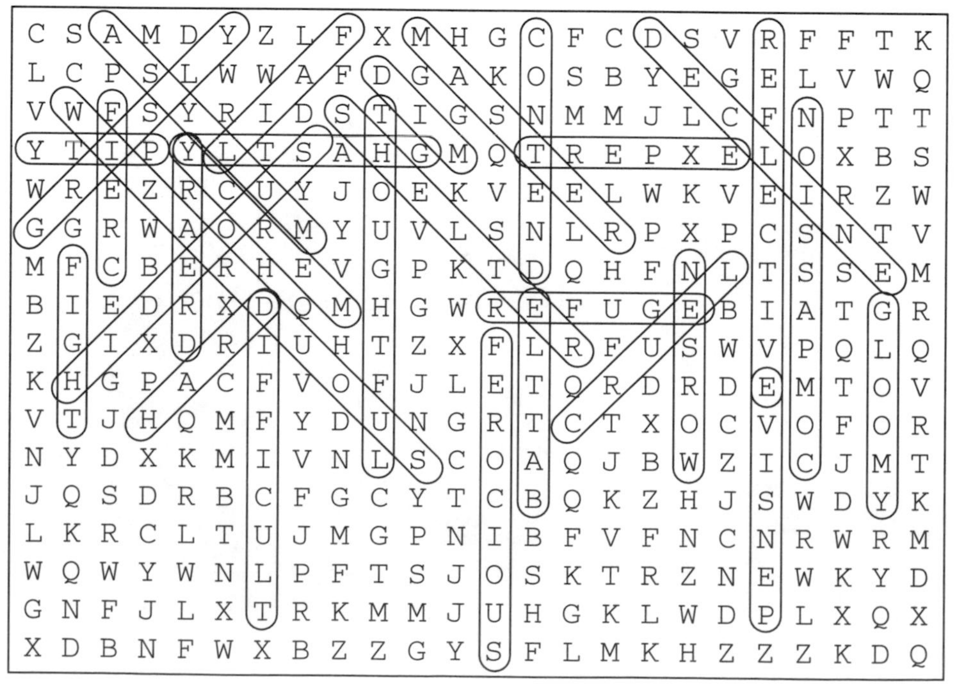

arduous; difficult; hard
asylum; refuge; shelter
battle; contend; fight
compassion; mercy; pity
cruel; ferocious; fierce
decline; fail; worsen
dim; dreary; gloomy
expert; master; wizard
ghastly; grisly; hideous
pensive; reflective; thoughtful

## 1-81. CONNECTING THE PREFIX AND THE ROOT

1. absence
2. ambulance
3. antecedent
4. monarchy
5. benefit
6. biography
7. chronicle
8. democracy
9. diction
10. erratic
11. deflect
12. progress
13. hyperactive
14. hypodermic
15. malfunction
16. novice
17. pedestrian
18. portfolio
19. prolific
20. psychology
21. retrorocket
22. separate
23. sequence
24. invert
25. video

## 1-82. YOU : WINNER

| | | | |
|---|---|---|---|
| A = 4 | B = 6 | C = 11 | D = 13 |
| E = 9 | F = 15 | G = 2 | H = 8 |
| I = 14 | J = 12 | K = 5 | L = 3 |
| M = 7 | N = 1 | O = 16 | P = 10 |

# 1-83. START WITH A VOWEL

**Across**
1. ODD
3. OCEAN
7. UGLY
8. OBSERVE
10. AUTUMN
11. ULNA
12. EVIL
13. URANUS
15. ASK
16. UTAH
17. OMEGA
19. ILL
21. ITEM
22. ANGUISH
24. INFLATE
26. ORB
27. ATOM
28. EMPTY
29. APPOINT
30. EXTREME

**Down**
1. OPTION
2. ELEVEN
3. OWL
4. EVACUATE
5. ASSIST
6. URBAN
7. UNUSUAL
8. OMEN
9. EXHALE
10. ARK
11. UNITED
14. AUDIO
17. OTTAWA
18. AROMA
20. IMPROVE
22. AUGUST
23. INTREPID
24. IMPORT
25. ENAMEL
27. AUNT

# 1-84. SOMETHING IN COMMON

| 1 D | | 2 Q | U | 3 E | S | 4 T | I | O | N | 5 M | A | R | K | | | 6 P | | | | | | | |
|---|---|---|---|---|---|---|---|---|---|---|---|---|---|---|---|---|---|---|---|---|---|---|---|
| A | | | | T | | I | | | | E | | | | 7 D | U | E | T | | 8 K | | | | |
| 9 S | U | 10 L | K | Y | | R | | | | 11 M | O | U | S | E | | R | | | E | | | | |
| H | | A | | M | | E | | | | O | | | | F | | 12 I | N | D | E | X | | | |
| | | B | | O | | | 13 S | T | E | R | N | | | I | | O | | | L | | | | |
| | | O | | L | | | E | | | Y | | | | N | | D | | | | | | | 14 G |
| | | R | | O | | | R | | | | 15 C | H | A | I | N | | | | 16 C | | | | L |
| | | E | | G | | | G | | 17 H | | | | | T | | | | 18 B | O | W | | | O |
| | | R | | Y | | 19 P | E | D | A | L | | 20 C | L | I | F | F | | | R | | | | S |
| | 21 S | | | | 22 C | | A | | R | | | | | O | | | | | P | | 23 E | | S |
| | 24 C | A | 25 P | T | A | I | N | | D | | | 26 C | O | N | 27 C | E | R | T | O | | M | | A |
| | R | | A | | R | | T | | W | | | O | | | O | | | | R | | P | | R |
| | A | | D | | R | | | | A | | | L | | | M | | | 28 V | A | L | L | E | Y |
| | T | | D | | I | | | | R | | 29 B | U | S | | M | | | | L | | O | | |
| | C | | O | | A | | 30 S | L | E | D | | M | | | 31 A | R | I | A | | | Y | | |
| | H | | C | | G | | | | | | | N | | | | | | | | | E | | |
| | | | K | | E | | | | | | | | | | | | | | | | E | | |

## 1-85. END WHERE YOU BEGAN

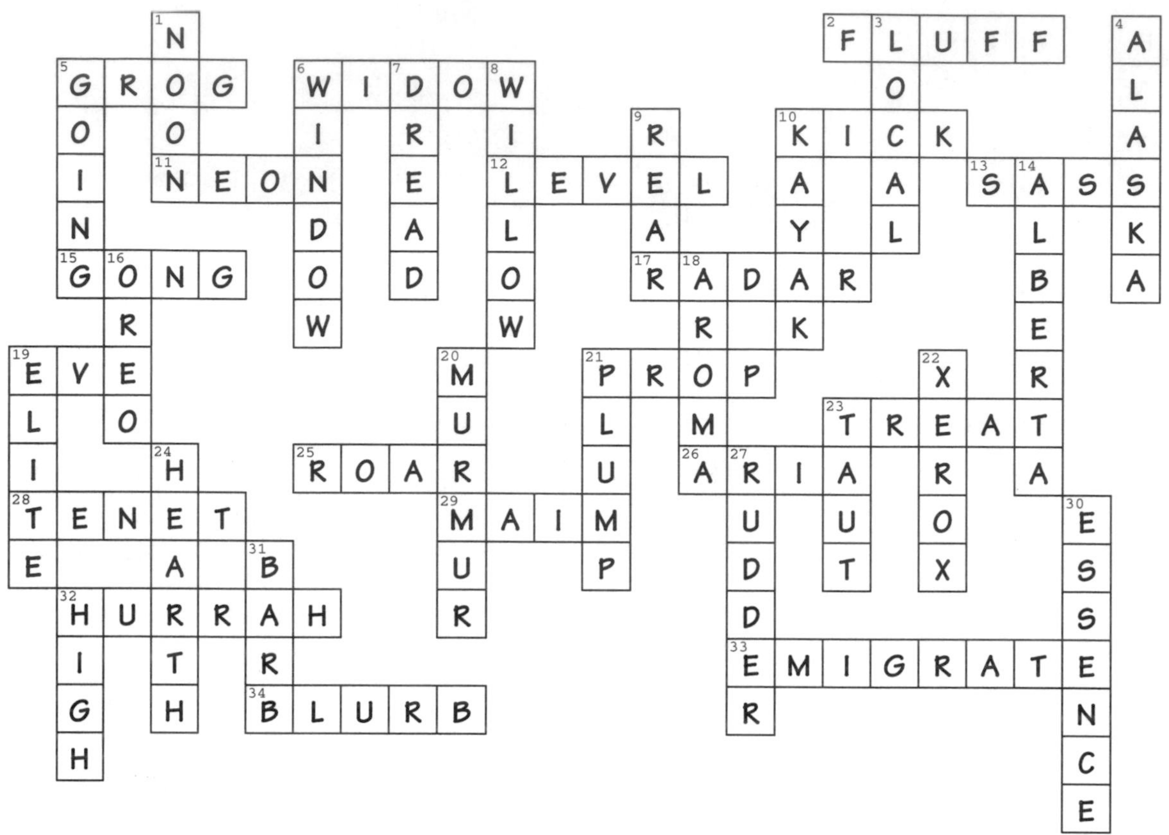

## 1-86. X MARKS THE SPOT

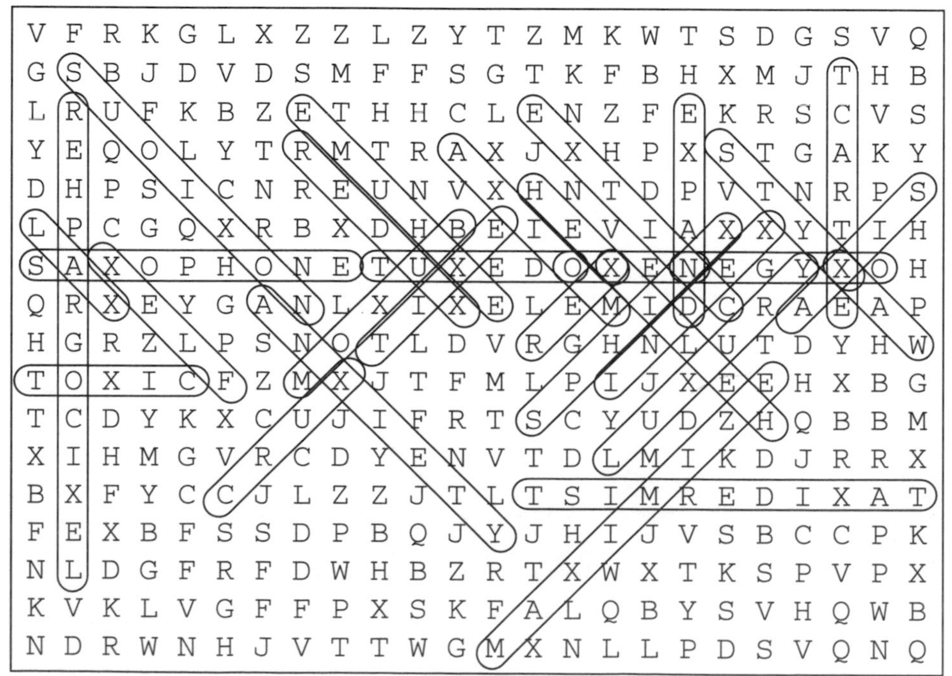

| | | | | |
|---|---|---|---|---|
| ANXIETY | EXIT | HEX | NOXIOUS | SPHINX |
| AXIOM | EXPAND | INDEX | OXEN | STYX |
| AXIS | EXTINCT | LAX | OXYGEN | TAXIDERMIST |
| BUXOM | EXTRACT | LEXICOGRAPHER | REDUX | TOXIC |
| CRUX | FLEX | LUXURY | REX | TUXEDO |
| EXHUME | HELIX | MAXIMIZE | SAXOPHONE | WAX |

## 1-87. SMALL'S SYNONYMS

| | | | |
|---|---|---|---|
| 1. MINUSCULE | 6. THIN | 11. STUNTED | 16. LIMITED |
| 2. MINIATURE | 7. BRIEF | 12. MINUTE | 17. SLIGHT |
| 3. UNIMPORTANT | 8. TRIFLING | 13. LITTLE | 18. SLENDER |
| 4. PETITE | 9. REDUCED | 14. SPARE | 19. INSIGNIFICANT |
| 5. PUNY | 10. MINOR | 15. COMPACT | 20. INCONSEQUENTIAL |

Letter: A B C D E F G H I J K L M N O P Q R S T U V W X Y Z
Substitute: D R G I F N P M Y C O K W H Z E A J B U L S T V Q X

## 1-88. SYNONYMS FOR BIG

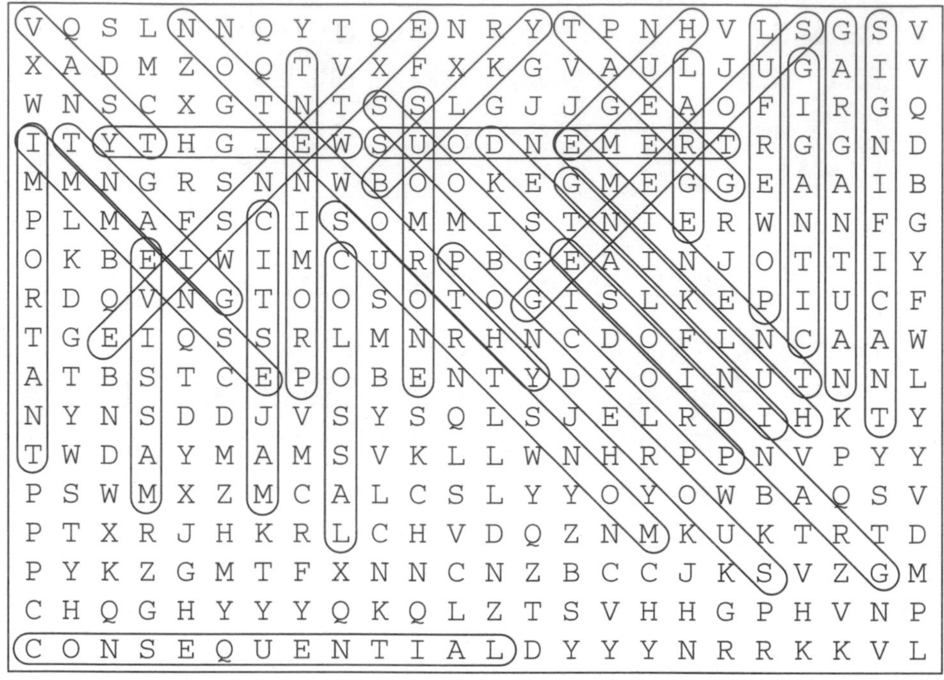

| | | | | |
|---|---|---|---|---|
| BULKY | GARGANTUAN | HUGE | MAJESTIC | PRODIGIOUS |
| COLOSSAL | GENEROUS | HULKING | MASSIVE | PROMINENT |
| CONSEQUENTIAL | GIANT | INFLATED | MONSTROUS | SIGNIFICANT |
| EMINENT | GIGANTIC | IMMENSE | NOTEWORTHY | TREMENDOUS |
| ENORMOUS | GRANDIOSE | IMPORTANCE | PONDEROUS | VAST |
| EXTENSIVE | GREAT | LARGE | POWERFUL | WEIGHTY |

## 1-89. SYNONYMS FOR TALK

1. LECTURE
2. ADDRESS
3. ARTICULATE
4. SERMONIZE
5. PARLEY
6. GOSSIP
7. CONSULT
8. PREACH
9. COMMUNICATE
10. ORATE
11. PONTIFICATE
12. SPEAK
13. EXPRESS
14. TELL
15. CHATTER
16. CONFER
17. PROCLAIM
18. DECLAIM
19. SAY
20. CHAT

*Letter:* A B C D E F G H I J K L M N O P Q R S T U V W X Y Z
*Code:* U I K S F L W E P M R A X V C J P Y T D G Z O H Q N

# 1-90. THREE'S COMPANY

1. RIDICULE / RIDICULOUS
2. LURE
3. UNIQUE
4. NOBLE
5. UNCLEAR
6. UNCERTAIN
7. PROMISE
8. WARRANT
9. ROYAL
10. IDIOTIC
11. FALSE / FAKE
12. SUGGES
13. PLEDGE
14. PROFFER
15. FOOLISH
16. RELIABLE
17. KINGLY
18. TEASE
19. IDEAL
20. SATIRIZE / SEPARATE
21. VAGUE
22. LOYAL
23. TRUE
24. ENTICE
25. PARODY
26. OFFER
27. SPURIOUS
28. ENTIRE
29. FLAWLESS
30. REMARKABLE